"In this helpful volume, Matthew Ma
ical hermeneutics and the practice o
location is a particularly welcomed co
tics to Exegesis for any who want to take the next step in their exploration of biblical
hermeneutics."

—*Jeannine K. Brown, professor of New Testament and director of online programs, Bethel
Seminary*

"In books about biblical interpretation, it is easy to lose sight of the canonical and Christological forest for the weeds of steps, methods, and tools. *From Hermeneutics to Exegesis*
is a welcome exception to this tendency in hermeneutics texts. Matthew Malcolm eru-
ditely sets the tools of exegesis in the larger context of Scripture's Christological purpose,
reminding us that reading the Bible is done in order to see Christ with his Church, by his
Spirit. This book will help train the next generation of Christian ministers and interpreters
to exegete God's Word carefully and theologically. I highly recommend it for use in the
classroom and the church."

—*Matthew Y. Emerson, Dickinson associate professor of religion, Oklahoma Baptist University*

"Hermeneutics is not just a long term designed to confuse those interested in the Bible. As Mathew Malcolm clearly illustrates in this surprisingly complete introduction
to hermeneutics, interpretation, and exegesis, hermeneutics is the essential beginning to
understanding that culminates in acts of interpretation and then useful exegesis. Malcolm
emphasizes the location of the text and of the reader and how they must enter into an
essential dialogue with each other. As a result, Malcolm bridges the gap between general
and special hermeneutics and arrives at an informed and workable approach to interpretation of the Bible. I recommend this book for its timeliness, currency, and helpfulness."

—*Stanley E. Porter, president and dean, McMaster Divinity College, Canada*

"I am delighted to commend this book without reserve. Matthew Malcolm combines academic expertise with exceptional down-to-earth common sense. He is equally competent
in biblical studies, theology, and broader questions about interpretation. I am especially
impressed by his thoughtful questions addressed to readers, which are stimulating, relevant and thought-provoking. He discusses many topics, including openness, expectation
and multifaceted interpretation. We shall doubtless hear more of Malcolm as an able
biblical scholar and theologian."

—*Anthony Thiselton, emeritus professor of Christian Theology, University of Nottingham,
U.K.*

From

HERMENEUTICS

to

EXEGESIS

From

HERMENEUTICS

to

EXEGESIS

The Trajectory
of Biblical
Interpretation

MATTHEW R. MALCOLM

ACADEMIC

NASHVILLE, TENNESSEE

From Hermeneutics to Exegisis
Copyright © 2018 by Matthew Malcolm

Published by B&H Academic
Nashville, Tennessee
All rights reserved.

ISBN: 978-1-4627-4377-3

Dewey Decimal Classification: 220.6
Subject Heading: BIBLE--CRITICISM

The web addresses referenced in this book were live and correct at the time of the book's publication but may be subject to change.

Cover design credits: Christ Pantocrator, 1607 (oil on panel), Bulgarian School, (17th century) / National Art Gallery, Sofia, Bulgaria / Bridgeman Images Cover design credit also goes to *Darren Welch*

Printed in the United States of America
2 3 4 5 6 7 8 9 10 SB 23 22 21 20 19

To two fine linguists, educationalists,
and Christian interpreters:
my parents,
Ian and Kaye Malcolm

CONTENTS

ACKNOWLEDGMENTS

I first gained an interest in the field of hermeneutics through the influence of my doctoral supervisor, Anthony Thiselton. I continue to be grateful to him for his constantly stimulating work and his kind help. His influence on my thought will be plain to anyone familiar with his important contributions to this topic.

I developed much of the material that formed the basis of this book when I had the opportunity to develop a master's class on hermeneutics for the Australian College of Theology. I am grateful for that opportunity and for the wonderful students to whom I taught hermeneutics at Trinity Theological College in Western Australia.

I am thankful for the many opportunities at my present university for stimulating interaction with students, fellow faculty members, and outsiders. I particularly appreciate the important discussions that occur in the "All That Teak" study group. These serve to provoke my hermeneutical horizons, sharpen my thought, and improve my scholarship.

I am grateful to those who took the time to read through my manuscript and offer me constructive feedback. Particular thanks go to Matthew Emerson, as well as my parents, to whom this book is dedicated. As always, I am grateful to my wife and children, through whom I am blessed to have my own horizons pleasantly enlarged.

PREFACE

D o you have eyes and not see?" an exasperated Jesus asked his disciples, who had failed to understand him yet again. This book is designed to help serious students of biblical literature reflect on how they can interpret the Bible with eyes that are open. As the title indicates, the book gives attention first to the field of hermeneutics (which is more abstract), and then to the practice of exegesis (which is more applied). This means that the opening chapters are more theoretical and intellectually challenging, but are designed to provide a solid grounding that will pay off later in the book.

Since this is an academic textbook, the style is scholarly; but given that a feature of the field of hermeneutics is an acknowledgment of the locatedness of authors and readers, I do not try to conceal my own individuality behind a detached façade. In other words, I try to be open about the fact that this book is written by a particular person and therefore carries my own viewpoints and is indebted to my own scholarly heritage. At the same time, I hope it will be stimulating and useful for a wide range of readers.

Indeed, the topic this book addresses is of crucial significance throughout the world at this time. As I write this, my own part of the world is in a state of unprecedented hermeneutical controversy, as a famous Christian has just been imprisoned for his public interpretation of a Muslim text. In other parts of the world, claims about religious convictions, biblical texts, and their impacts on politics are rife in public discussion. It is essential at such a time that there be contributors to public conversation who are resourced by deep, rigorous reflection on the nature of understanding and its application to biblical texts.

Developing an understanding of hermeneutics and gaining skills in exegesis will pay off in far broader ways as well, from making one a more insightful movie-watcher to improving one's skills in cross-disciplinary dialogue. But of course, many readers of this book will be interested in applying interpretation of the Bible to Christian ministry. I encourage such readers not to jump immediately to the practical ideas on exegesis, but to take the time to work through the theoretical chapters as well. As a whole, the book aims to help readers become more attentive, and more self-aware, interpreters. To these readers I offer the exhortation of the Venerable Bede, which comes from the close of an amazing homily about reading Scripture:

> Let us make the strong vessels of our hearts clean by faith . . . and let us fill them with the waters of saving knowledge by paying attention more frequently to sacred reading. Let us ask the Lord that the grace of knowledge which he has conferred upon us may not chance to puff us up, that it warm us with the fervor of his charity. . . . And so it comes about that to us also, if we are making good progress, Jesus may manifest his glory both now in a partial way, insofar as we are capable of grasping it, and in the future perfectly.[1]

---

[1] Homily 1.14 in Bede the Venerable, *Homilies on the Gospels: Book One: Advent to Lent,* trans. Lawrence T. Martin and David Hurst OSB (Kalamazoo: Cistercian, 1991), 145–46.

1

UNDERSTANDING HERMENEUTICS AND EXEGESIS

In this chapter, we will ponder the meaning and significance of hermeneutics and exegesis. This will introduce concepts and raise questions that we will consider throughout the rest of the book.

The Relevance of Hermeneutics

The Church of the Nativity in Bethlehem has a stone doorway that is about waist height. This entry is intentionally too low for people to be able to walk straight in. I have sometimes shown a photo of this doorway to my students and asked them, "Is this doorway designed to let people in or to keep people out?" The answer, quite brilliantly, is that it is designed to let in those who are willing to bow down, but obstruct those who refuse. It is intended to welcome those who are willing to stoop to the stature of a child, while infuriating those with heads held high (to use a biblical phrase; see: Isa 3:16).

The question I ask my students about the doorway could also be asked of Jesus's parables: Are they designed to let people in or to keep people out? Jesus seemed to suggest the latter when he directly addressed this issue in Mark 4:11–12: "Everything comes in parables so that they may indeed look, and yet not perceive; they may indeed listen, and yet not understand; otherwise, they might turn back and be forgiven."

But notice that Jesus only expected this reaction from those with heads held high—the self-positioned "outsiders." Verse 11 begins, "He answered them [his disciples], 'The secret of the kingdom of God has been given to you, but to those outside, everything comes in parables so that . . .'"

Jesus went on to show that he expected his disciples, unlike these outsiders, to understand the parables—because they were following the One the parables reveal. Mark 4:13 reads, "Then he said to them: 'Don't you understand this parable? How then will you understand all of the parables?'"

This parable—like the church doorway—appears the same to everyone. But it is designed to have a very different impact on those who approach it as "insiders" versus those who read it as "outsiders." The insiders are expected to be able to interpret and understand it, resulting in new riches of appreciation for their Lord. But for the "stiff-necked" outsiders,[1] the parable will confuse and confound the knowledge of Jesus they appear to possess. Mark 4:24–25 says, "Pay attention to what you hear. By the measure you use, it will be measured to you—and more will be added to you. For whoever has, more will be given to him, and whoever does not have, even what he has will be taken away from him."

It would seem that according to Jesus, reaching understanding—arriving at a right interpretation—is not simply a matter of decoding grammar and syntax. Some of those who did this right and were personally familiar with Jesus's first-century cultural context still found themselves hopelessly lost.

Let us move on a little further in Mark's Gospel to see another story where Jesus explicitly dealt with issues of interpretation. In Mark 8, shortly after the disciples witnessed the miraculous feeding of the four thousand, we read:

> The disciples had forgotten to take bread and had only one loaf with them in the boat. Then he gave them strict orders: "Watch out! Beware of the leaven of the Pharisees and the leaven of Herod." They were discussing among themselves that they did not have any bread. Aware of this, he said to them, "Why are you discussing the fact you have no bread? Don't you understand or comprehend? Do you have hardened hearts? Do you have eyes and not see; do you have ears and not hear?" (vv. 14–18)

The disciples had failed to interpret Jesus's words effectively. And he saw their lack of understanding as arising from *who they were*: they were people in danger of having hardened hearts. So how might their hearts be softened? Jesus went on to show them that certain past events should have positioned them to interpret his words effectively:

---

[1] Here I am borrowing a term God used again and again to describe Israel. See Exod 32:9; 33:3, 5; 34:9, among others.

"Do you not remember? When I broke the five loaves for the five thousand, how many baskets full of leftovers did you collect?"

"Twelve," they told him.

"When I broke the seven loaves for the four thousand, how many baskets full of pieces did you collect?"

"Seven," they said.

And he said to them, "Don't you understand yet?" (vv. 18–21)

But notice that Jesus was withholding crucial information from them. Notice that he didn't say, "Remember how, in Jewish territory, I created twelve basketfuls of leftover bread—and that twelve is symbolic of Israel? And remember when I met that Gentile woman who asked for leftover crumbs of bread, and I subsequently went to Gentile territory and created seven basketfuls of leftover bread? And remember how seven is symbolic of wholeness or universality? Did you notice that, whereas Moses fed exactly the right amount of manna to the people of Israel, I provided abundant leftovers, even for those outside Israel? And don't you remember that after I did these miraculous signs, the Pharisees immediately asked for a sign regarding my identity, and I refused them? And then I warned you to watch out for the leaven of the Pharisees! You *should* have realized that the 'leaven of the Pharisees' represents stubbornly refusing to acknowledge the signs that bear witness to me as the promised provider who is greater than Moses!"

Jesus did not say any of this. He clearly wanted his disciples to read between the lines of his words and actions, if they were to be effective interpreters. They needed to be people with soft hearts, rightly attentive to the symbolic significance of certain things he said and did. It would seem that according to Jesus, interpretation is more than the objective analysis of words and sentences.

Let us consider one more passage. In Mark 9 we read, "He was teaching his disciples and telling them, 'The Son of Man is going to be betrayed into the hands of men. They will kill him, and after he is killed, he will rise three days later.' But they did not understand this statement, and they were afraid to ask him" (vv. 31–32).

Given that Jesus seemed to be speaking plainly here, it is worth asking why the disciples did not understand him. Is it because their hearts hadn't sufficiently softened? Is it because they had only begun to see who Jesus was, but were still at the stage of semi-sight, in which things resembled "trees walking" (8:24)? Even so, why did this impact their ability to interpret a straightforward, nonpoetic statement? It seems that once again, *where people are*—their "locatedness," to use a term that will become important—impacts the nature of their interpretation and understanding, whether they are facing parables, ambiguous sayings, or even apparently straightforward statements.

These moments in the Gospel of Mark illustrate the importance of considering what is involved when people seek to understand and effectively interpret the Bible. This, precisely, is the interest of this book.

Definitions of *Hermeneutics* and *Exegesis*

What Is Hermeneutics?

The twentieth century German scholar who is regarded as the father of philosophical hermeneutics, Hans-Georg Gadamer, wrote, "Hermeneutics is above all a practice, the art of understanding."[2] I think this is an excellent general encapsulation. But can we be more precise? There are problems in defining *hermeneutics*—especially in the context of biblical studies—because it is used in at least five different ways.

There is the *popular Christian usage*, in which hermeneutics is said to refer to the application of exegesis. Theologians Gordon D. Fee and Douglas Stuart, in their book *How to Read the Bible for All Its Worth*, remark, "Proper 'hermeneutics' begins with solid exegesis."[3] According to this conception, one begins by exegeting or interpreting the text, and then moves to the hermeneutical stage of considering how one's exegesis ought to be applied in today's world. An endorsement for Fee and Stuart's book on the publisher's blog states, "Remember: start with exegesis and follow up with hermeneutics. Reverse the order and you risk not reading the Bible for all its worth."[4]

There is also the *exegetical handbook usage*, in which hermeneutics is seen as being similar to interpretation, but perhaps broader in scope. Authors Andreas Köstenberger and Richard Patterson seem to equate interpretation with hermeneutics, as they have commented on their "quest of sound biblical interpretation or as it is also called, 'hermeneutics.'"[5] In this view, then, hermeneutics means the interpretation of texts in accordance with proper principles or rules.

---

[2] Hans-Georg Gadamer, quoted in Anthony C. Thiselton, *Hermeneutics: An Introduction* (Grand Rapids: Eerdmans, 2009), 2.

[3] Gordon D. Fee and Douglas Stuart, *How to Read the Bible for All Its Worth*, 2nd ed. (Grand Rapids: Zondervan, 2003), 25.

[4] Jeremy Bouma, "Exegesis and Hermeneutics: The Bible Interpreter's Two Most Important Tasks," Zondervan Academic blog, July 8, 2014, http://zondervanacademic.com/blog/biblical-interpretation-exegesis-and-hermeneutics/.

[5] Andreas J. Köstenberger and Richard D. Patterson, *Invitation to Biblical Interpretation: Exploring the Hermeneutical Triad of History, Literature, and Theology* (Grand Rapids: Kregel, 2011), 57.

Then there is the *popular theological usage*, in which "a hermeneutic" (singular) is regarded as a particular interpretive approach that is used in a certain instance or by a certain interpreter. So, someone might be said to utilize a "liberation hermeneutic" or a "hermeneutic of suspicion."

In the *academic/philosophical usage*, "hermeneutics" refers to abstract reflection on universal conditions for interpretation or understanding. This use of the term does not generally involve a context in which particular principles or rules for interpretation are being sought or advocated. Rather, it involves a consideration of the factors that are inevitably at play when interpretation occurs.

Finally, there is the broader *cultural analytical usage*, in which hermeneutic(s) refers to a mode of being that prioritizes listening, interpretation, and understanding. For example, in the field of international education, you might hear something like this: "During [the hermeneutic stage of comparative education studies] comparative educationists attempted to understand (i.e. interpret) national education systems from within the national context in which they functioned."[6]

The fact that the term *hermeneutics* can mean so many things in different contexts can result (perhaps ironically) in major miscommunication and misunderstanding. If someone is advocating the importance of hermeneutics in the field of biblical studies, is he suggesting that it is important to apply the Bible sensitively in today's world or that people should make use of proper interpretive methods? If someone vigorously denies that "general hermeneutics" should feature in biblical interpretation, is she denying that a general set of rules should be used for interpreting all Bible passages or saying that biblical scholars should examine the factors that inevitably impact all interpretation?

I use the differentiation in terms provided by Thiselton, which fits with the academic/philosophical usage I just described: "Whereas *exegesis* and *interpretation* denote the *actual processes* of interpreting texts, *hermeneutics* also includes the second-order discipline of *asking critically what exactly we are doing when we read, understand, or apply* texts. Hermeneutics explores the *conditions and criteria* that operate to try to ensure responsible, valid, fruitful, or appropriate interpretation."[7]

> *Hermeneutics means the study of what is happening when effective interpretation or understanding takes place.*

---

[6] C. C. Wolhuter, "The Development of Comparative Education," in C. C. Wolhuter, E. M. Lemmer, and N. C. de Wet, eds., *Comparative Education: Education Systems and Contemporary Issues* (Pretoria, ZA: Van Schaik, 2007), 5–6.

[7] Thiselton, *Hermeneutics*, 4; emphases in original.

It is crucial to see, according to this definition, that the aim of hermeneutics is not to apply rules of interpretation, but to explore what is happening when fruitful understanding takes place. This is different from some "hermeneutics" handbooks, such as Köstenberger and Patterson's volume, titled *Invitation to Biblical Interpretation*, which is explicitly about recognizing proper "rules": "It is this authorial intention the interpreter must aim to recover. . . . When my wife talks to me, I dare not give her words my own preferred meaning. The rules of proper communication demand that I seek to understand the meaning *she* intended to convey."[8]

Similarly, see New Testament scholar Grant R. Osborne's discussion of "laws" of interpretation: "Hermeneutics is a science, since it provides a logical, orderly classification of the laws of interpretation."[9]

Again, the place of hermeneutics as defined by Thiselton is not to spell out rules or laws such as these, but to explore the various factors at work when fruitful communication and understanding take place—particularly with regard to texts.

What Is Exegesis?

I regard exegesis as intentional, attentive, respectful interpretation of a particular written text. This does not mean that an exegete has to be sympathetic to the content of the text being interpreted; it simply means that the exegete will seek to fairly hear, analyze, and flesh out the content of a passage of text. It is a labored formalization of that which ideally takes place automatically for an attuned hearer. While exegesis can be conducted on any text, the word itself is usually used to refer to analysis of biblical texts.

Given that this book seeks to move "from hermeneutics to exegesis," we will come to further define *exegesis* later on, in chapter 8.

Images of Hermeneutics and Exegesis

You may have come across different images of "hermeneutics" or "exegesis."

A Circle?

One very common image is the "hermeneutical circle." This image came to the fore with German theologian Friedrich Schleiermacher in the early nineteenth

---

[8] Köstenberger and Patterson, *Invitation to Biblical Interpretation*, 58.

[9] Grant R. Osborne, *The Hermeneutical Spiral: A Comprehensive Introduction to Biblical Interpretation*, rev. and exp. (Downers Grove, IL: IVP Academic, 2006), 21. Osborne also adds that hermeneutics is an art, since it must be imaginatively applied, and that it is spiritual, since (for biblical interpretation) it is dependent on the Holy Spirit.

century. Schleiermacher commented, "Complete knowledge is always in this apparent circle, that each particular can only be understood via the general, of which it is a part, and vice versa. And every piece of knowledge is only scientific if it is formed in this way."[10]

The circle represents the conviction that it is inevitable that any process of understanding or interpretation will move from a general sense of the whole to a particular analysis of a part, which in turn will refine one's general sense of the whole—which will further influence one's particular analysis of an individual part. This circle continues around as the interpreter progresses in understanding.

A Spiral?

But some find that the image of a circle sounds too . . . circular. It may give the impression of being endlessly unproductive. So some prefer the image of a spiral. But note that this image is not always used in the same way as the circle. Grant Osborne has proposed that

> biblical interpretation entails a "spiral" from text to context, from its original meaning to its contextualization or significance for the church today. . . . I am not going round and round a closed circle that can never detect the true meaning but am spiraling nearer and nearer to the text's intended meaning as I refine my hypotheses and allow the text to continue to challenge and correct those alternative interpretations, then to guide my delineation of its significance for my situation today.[11]

Notice that for Osborne, the spiral is not between "whole" and "part" (as in the hermeneutical circle), but between "original meaning" and "contextualization" today.

A Triad?

Köstenberger and Patterson propose the image of a triad: "Those who want to succeed in the task of biblical interpretation need to proceed within a proper interpretive framework, that is, the hermeneutical triad, which consists of the three elements interpreters must address in studying any given biblical passage

---

[10] Friedrich Schleiermacher, "Hermeneutics and Criticism," in *Hermeneutics and Criticism and Other Writings*, trans. Andrew Bowie, Cambridge Texts in the History of Philosophy (Cambridge: Cambridge University Press, 1998), 24.
[11] Osborne, *The Hermeneutical Spiral*, 22.

regardless of its genre: a book's *historical setting* . . . , its *literary dimension* . . . , and its *theological message*."[12]

Köstenberger and Patterson's triad of history, literature, and theology seems close to the common concern of interpreters to look *behind* the text (at its background and contexts), *in* the text (at its literary features), and *in front* of the text (at its impacts).

Horizons?

A well-known image that comes from the field of philosophical hermeneutics is that of "horizons," in which text and reader (or two other subjects) are seen as inhabiting separate locations, which are able to be enlarged and engaged. "Understanding takes place when the interpreter's horizons engage with those of the text. . . . Gadamer's image of a fusion of horizons provides one possible way of describing the main problem and task of hermeneutics."[13]

Each of these images has something to offer. In this book, we will be working with a model of hermeneutics that features the separate *horizons* of text and interpreter, and the productive *circle* of refining interpretation.

Outcomes of a Hermeneutical Encounter

What do we hope will come out of a "hermeneutical encounter"? Are we hoping to develop an encapsulated account from a textual portion's content? Do we hope for understanding? Or, are we aiming for transformation of ourselves or our culture? Are our aims fair? Are they appropriate? Are they sufficient? We will come to consider a goal for hermeneutics in chapter 6, but it is worth pondering this point at the outset.

In the meantime, another question presents itself: If hermeneutics does abstractly reflect upon—as Gadamer puts it—"the art of understanding," in order to appreciate what is happening when we seek to interpret, is it really possible for it to result in practical exegetical procedures? As academics Niall Keane and Chris Lawn have pointed out, Gadamer himself was suspicious of such practicality: "Far from teasing out the practical implications of hermeneutics, his real concern 'was

---

[12] Köstenberger and Patterson, *Invitation to Biblical Interpretation*, 65–66.
[13] Anthony C. Thiselton, *The Two Horizons: New Testament Hermeneutics and Philosophical Description* (Grand Rapids: Eerdmans, 1980), 16.

and is philosophic: not what we do or what we ought to do, but what happens to us over and above our wanting and doing.'"[14]

Is it then a betrayal of hermeneutics (in the academic/philosophical sense) to seek to move "from hermeneutics to exegesis"? I don't think so: it will be seen that this movement does not in fact mean collecting general rules from "hermeneutics" and then applying them to "exegesis." Rather, it will involve allowing an appreciation for the insights of hermeneutics to help us to conduct exegesis *with eyes that are open*—open to features such as the contexts of the text, our own locatedness as readers, our indebtedness to prior traditions of understanding, and the situations in which fruitful understanding frequently takes place.

> **BIG IDEA**
>
> Jesus himself indicated that numerous factors are at work when people seek to interpret the Bible. Hermeneutics involves abstract reflection on what is happening when fruitful interpretation and understanding occur. Exegesis is intentional, attentive, respectful interpretation of a particular written text.

Questions for Discussion

Consider again the questions that surface from Mark's presentation of Jesus. *Read Mark 4:12–13.*

- Did Jesus tell parables so that people would understand, or not?
- What seemed to be needed in order for the disciples to understand the parable?
- So, is "understanding" a matter of correctly analyzing grammar and syntax? Why or why not?

Read Mark 8:14–21.

- What resulted in a lack of understanding in 8:17?
- What seemed to be required for the disciples to understand the meaning of Jesus's statement about leaven?
- Reflect on what this reveals about how successful understanding takes place.

---

[14] Niall Keane and Chris Lawn, *The Blackwell Companion to Hermeneutics* (Chichester, UK: Wiley Blackwell, 2016), 6.

Read Mark 9:30–32.

- Jesus appeared to be speaking plainly here. So why did the disciples not understand?
- What would have enabled the disciples to understand?

Read Mark 13:14.

- What is meant by the parenthetical "let the reader understand"? Could you rephrase this instruction?
- Does the reader have a role, then, in contributing meaning? Are there other instances in which the reader might need to "understand" what is not explicitly said?
- What hermeneutical issues are raised, then, by Mark's presentation of Jesus?

For Further Reading

Introductions to Biblical Hermeneutics or Interpretation
Bartholomew, Craig G. 2015. *Introducing Biblical Hermeneutics.* Grand Rapids: Baker Academic.
Jasper, David. 2004. *A Short Introduction to Hermeneutics.* Louisville: Westminster John Knox Press.
Jensen, Alexander S. 2007. *Theological Hermeneutics.* London: SCM Press.
Reference Works on Hermeneutics as an Academic Discipline
Keane, Niall, and Chris Lawn, eds. 2016. *The Blackwell Companion to Hermeneutics* Chichester, UK: John Wiley & Sons.
Malpas, Jeff, and Hans-Helmuth Gander, eds. 2015. *The Routledge Companion to Hermeneutics.* Oxford, UK: Routledge.

2

THE HISTORY OF HERMENEUTICS, PART 1: SOCRATES TO ANGELA OF FOLIGNO

Hermeneutics as a discipline has arisen within Western theology and philosophy. For this reason, the historical moments we will be examining will especially relate to figures within these traditions, without meaning to imply that fruitful consideration of understanding and interpretation has not occurred in other settings. We will be considering both theorists and notable practitioners of the task of interpretation. As much as possible, I will allow these figures to speak in their own voices by drawing attention to key quotations from their own works.

This exploration is not intended to be exhaustive. My intention here is to draw attention to particular features that have gained a stable place in hermeneutical discussion today. (This chapter and the next are the heaviest in the book.)

Socrates and Plato

From the time of Socrates (469–399 BC), Western philosophy has shown interest in reflecting abstractly on how humans communicate and understand. In the works of Socrates' student Plato (420s–348 BC), a number of hermeneutical issues surface. Five are worth mentioning.

First, Plato recognized that the study of meaning is worth pursuing. In his *Cratylus*, Plato seems to advocate that everyday (Attic Greek) words are neither simply "natural" in communicating meaning, nor simply "conventional," but some mix of the two. That is, the names of objects do not arise automatically from the objects themselves, but neither are they purely up to the whims of societal convention. We will come back to this issue of how words communicate meaning when we discuss Augustine.

Second, Plato made a distinction between "truth" and "sophistry," with the recognition that hearers/readers may be manipulated by speakers/writers. Plato was famously suspicious of rhetoric and oratory, labeling rhetoric a sort of flattery that appeals to unvirtuous passions:

> What about the oratory addressed to the Athenian people and to those in other cities composed of free men? What is our view of this kind? Do you think that orators always speak with regard to what's best? Do they always set their sights on making the citizens as good as possible through their speeches? Or are they, too, bent upon the gratification of the citizens, and, slighting the common good for the sake of their own private good, do they treat the people like children, their sole attempt being to gratify them?[1]

Third, Plato held the conviction that perception is constrained by bodily locatedness. While for much later thinkers this could be viewed as a positive thing, for Plato it was an obstacle to true knowledge, because one's bodily locatedness brings with it inevitable biases and inaccuracies:[2]

> Then what about the actual acquiring of knowledge? Is the body an obstacle when one associates with it in the search for knowledge? I mean, for example, do men find any truth in sight or hearing, or are not even the poets forever telling us that we do not see or hear anything accurately, and surely if those two physical senses are not clear or precise, our other senses can hardly be accurate, as they are all inferior to these.[3]

> [I]nvestigation through the eyes is full of deceit, as is that through the ears and the other senses. Philosophy then persuades the soul to withdraw from the senses in so far as it is not compelled to use them.[4]

> [W]e have got to say that perception is one thing and knowledge another.[5]

---

[1] Plato, *Gorgias*, 502d–e, in John M. Cooper (ed.), *Plato: Complete Works* (Indianapolis: Hackett Publishing Company, 1997), 847.

[2] See the discussion of Heidegger and Gadamer that follows.

[3] Plato, *Phaedo*, 65a–b in Cooper, *Plato: Complete Works*, 56.

[4] Plato, *Phaedo*, 83a in Cooper, *Plato: Complete Works*, 72.

[5] Plato, *Theaetetus*, 164b in Cooper, *Plato: Complete Works*, 182.

Fourth, Plato recognized that authors—particularly creative writers—are not always fully self-aware. This raises the question of whether accessing "what was in the mind of the author" is actually the singular goal of interpretation:

> I went to the poets, the writers of tragedies and dithyrambs and the others. . . . So I took up those poems with which they seemed to have taken most trouble and asked them what they meant, in order that I might at the same time learn something from them. I am ashamed to tell you the truth, gentlemen, but I must. Almost all the bystanders might have explained the poems better than their authors could. I soon realized that poets do not compose their poems with knowledge, but by some inborn talent and by inspiration, like seers and prophets who also say many fine things without any understanding of what they say. The poets seemed to me to have had a similar experience.[6]

It is not just a postmodern view, then, that interpretation may mean going beyond the analysis of grammar or the intentions of the author. British theologian Brooke Foss Westcott, writing well before the turn to postmodernism, applied this insight to prophecy in the Bible. "No one would limit the teaching of a poet's words to that which was definitely present to his mind," he wrote. "Still less can we suppose that he who is inspired to give a message of GOD to all ages sees himself the completeness of the truth which all life serves to illuminate."[7]

On the other hand, Plato did not see the author's intentions as irrelevant, particularly in a philosophical debate. At one point, he imagined an interlocutor pleading with Socrates to pay attention to his intended meaning, rather than focusing narrowly on his wording: "I must beg you, this time, not to confine your attack to the letter of my doctrine," he said. "I am now going to make its meaning clearer to you."[8]

I was present at a conference on Psalms and the arts in St Andrews, Scotland, in 2009, during which the poet Michael Symmons Roberts spoke about his work. In the course of the discussion, someone from the floor pointed out that his poems frequently involve the idea of humans being tied to the earth, and Roberts himself appeared quite struck by this observation. It had not, apparently, been consciously articulated in his intentions, though he affirmed the observation with some delight.

---

[6] Plato, *Apology*, 22b–c in Cooper, *Plato: Complete Works*, 22.
[7] Brooke Foss Westcott, *The Epistle to the Hebrews: The Greek Text with Notes and Essays*, 3rd ed. (London: MacMillan, 1906), vii.
[8] Plato, *Theaetetus*, 166e; Cooper, 185.

Fifth, Plato suspected that words, once released from the pen of their author, are able to take on a life of their own. Unlike certain postmodern thinkers, he saw this as a negative thing:

> Writing shares a strange feature with painting. The offsprings of painting stand there as if they are alive, but if anyone asks them anything, they remain most solemnly silent. The same is true of written words. You'd think they were speaking as if they had some understanding, but if you question anything that has been said because you want to learn more, it continues to signify just that very same thing forever. When it has once been written down, every discourse roams about everywhere, reaching indiscriminately those with understanding no less than those who have no business with it, and it doesn't know to whom it should speak and to whom it should not. And when it is faulted and attacked unfairly, it always needs its father's support; alone, it can neither defend itself nor come to its own support.[9]

For this reason, Plato's Socrates argued that the path to knowledge comes through discussion with the wise, rather than through written texts. Fittingly, Plato's own literary output takes the form of *dialogues* (or "dialectic"),[10] in which various interlocutors (usually including Socrates) reach communal understanding. Hans-Georg Gadamer reflected on Plato's lasting contribution: "Now in this essence of dialectic . . . Plato discovers a characteristically positive quality; and this, precisely, is his accomplishment."[11]

Augustine and Chrysostom

Christian Writers before Augustine and Chrysostom

Early Christian writings are important in showing us how practitioners apply certain hermeneutical impulses to their interpretation of biblical texts. These impulses draw at times upon the heritage of interpretive instincts within the Old and New Testaments themselves, and also upon literary and rhetorical values of Hellenistic and Roman culture.

---

[9] Plato, *Phaedrus*, 275d–e in Cooper, *Plato: Complete Works*, 552.

[10] This is particularly true of Plato's early and middle works.

[11] Hans-Georg Gadamer, *Plato's Dialectical Ethics: Phenomenological Interpretations Relating to the Philebus*, trans. Robert M. Wallace (New Haven, CT: Yale University Press, 1991 [German 1983; first edition 1931]), 19.

Catholic theologian Lewis Ayres points out that in the late second century, Christian exegetes began to adopt Hellenistic techniques of literary analysis. He proposes that this occurred due to a struggle between emerging orthodoxy and Valentinian exegesis. The latter emphasized enigma, mystery, and secrecy as intentional elements of New Testament texts, which could be unlocked by skilled interpreters. In explicating these motifs in the New Testament, Valentinians drew on time-honored elements of Hellenistic literary analysis to lend weight to their interpretations. In response, Irenaeus (130–202) argued that the Valentinians were misunderstanding and misusing the literary techniques they sought to employ. Irenaeus insisted that the biblical texts were "plain" (*phaneros*), and that nonliteral or allegorical readings, which were sometimes appropriate, needed to be given proper justification.[12]

This interest in appropriately using Hellenistic interpretive techniques, including suitably justified use of symbolism and allegory, went on to become a feature of various strands of early Christian interpretation. For many, as with Irenaeus, the techniques would be adopted alongside a hermeneutical conviction that the one God had spoken plainly in the singular narrative of salvation that focused on Jesus.

Frances Young, a British theologian, captured the traditional distinction between "Alexandrian" and "Antiochene" exegesis:

> The exegetes of the third and fourth centuries inherited a body of traditional interpretations, notably those that understood Old Testament texts as prophecy of New Testament fulfillments. Their contribution was to introduce more systematic methods, to produce running commentaries, and to engage in discussion of what we would now call hermeneutical principles: thus the Antiochenes in the fourth century challenged the allegorical approach adopted by the Alexandrians in the third.[13]

As Young noted, this distinction is often overplayed and misunderstood. However, she does see the Antiochenes as more interested in the straightforward meaning of a text (*historia*) than their Alexandrian counterparts, who at times were overly taken with the text's inspired symbolic value.

---

[12] Lewis Ayres, "Irenaeus vs the Valentinians: Toward a Rethinking of Patristic Exegetical Origins," *Journal of Early Christian Studies* 23, no. 2 (July 2015): 153–87; http://dro.dur.ac.uk/12423/.
[13] Frances Young, "Alexandrian and Antiochene Exegesis," in Alan J. Hauser and Duane F. Watson, eds., *A History of Biblical Interpretation,* vol. 1, *The Ancient Period* (Grand Rapids: Eerdmans, 2003), 334.

Donald Fairbairn, of Gordon-Conwell Theological Seminary, noted that the old assumption was that for the (so-called Antiochene) patristics, "exegesis was the horse that pulled the theological cart."[14] But he went on to explain a movement away from this view in patristic scholarship: "Rather than asserting that exegesis was the horse pulling the theological cart, as the older view did, more recent scholarship has insisted that to a great degree, theology was the horse and exegesis the cart. More specifically, patristic exegesis, according to recent patristics scholars, was a task of reading all of Scripture in light of a controlling theological idea."[15]

This is the case for those characterized as "Antiochene" as much as for those characterized as "Alexandrian." They were gripped by the idea that the coming of Jesus Christ had redirected history—and they believed that this central theological truth should be heard echoing throughout Scripture and changing the lives of its hearers. Fairbairn cites the late Rowan A. Greer, a patristic scholar: "The theological traditions, derived themselves from Scripture, determine the questions asked of the text."[16]

Patristic writers are indeed up front and unapologetic about their reading mission, as proponents of the gospel of Jesus Christ. In examining Jonah as prefiguring Christ, Cyril of Alexandria commented, "Thus just as bees in the field, when flitting about the flowers, always gather up what is useful for the provision of the hives, so we also, when searching in the divinely inspired Scriptures, need always to be collecting and collating what is perfect for explicating Christ's mysteries and to interpret the Word fully without cause for rebuke."[17]

Stephen Wright, of Spurgeon's College (London), speaking with respect to premodern interpretation of the parables, wrote:

> They were treating the text as a sacred document through which *God* had revealed himself. They were interpreting it for the *divine meaning*. . . .

---

[14] Donald Fairbairn, 'Patristic Exegesis and Theology: The Cart and the Horse,' *Westminster Theological Journal* 69 (2007): 3.

[15] Ibid., 10.

[16] Fairbairn, "Patristic Exegesis," 12.

[17] Cyril of Alexandria, fragment 162, cited in Mark Sheridan, *Language for God in Patristic Tradition: Wrestling with Biblical Anthropomorphism* (Downers Grove, IL: IVP Academic, 2015), 85.

The didactic setting seems to have been one of the chief motivating forces behind the "allegorical" approach: the aim was to show how the parables illuminated Christian doctrine and contemporary life.[18]

It should be acknowledged that patristic biblical interpreters of all sorts were able to apply their hermeneutical instincts about the centrality of Christ in ways that sometimes leave present-day interpreters wincing. Young commented: "In practice drawing a line between typology and allegory in early Christian literature is impossible."[19]

Augustine

Augustine (354–430) is a towering figure not only for his interpretation of the Bible, but also for his stepping back to reflect abstractly on hermeneutical issues.

Like others before him, he was guided by his theological convictions in his exegesis of biblical texts. In particular, he understood the Old and New Testaments to come to a climax in the person of Jesus Christ and held that the moral impact of the Scriptures will be love for God and neighbor:

> We have repeatedly shown at great length, that the precepts and symbols of the Old Testament contained both what was to be fulfilled in obedience through the grace bestowed in the New Testament, and what was to be set aside as a proof of its having been fulfilled in the truth now made manifest. . . . By the precept men [in the Old Testament] were led, through a sense of guilt, to desire salvation; by the promise they were led to find in the typical observances the assurance that the Saviour would come.[20]

> Whoever, then, thinks that he understands the Holy Scriptures, or any part of them, but puts such an interpretation upon them as does not tend to build up this twofold love of God and our neighbor, does not yet understand them as he ought.[21]

---

[18] Stephen I. Wright, *The Voice of Jesus: Studies in the Interpretation of Six Gospel Parables* (Milton Keynes, UK: Paternoster, 2007), 63, 66.

[19] Young, "Alexandrian and Antiochene Exegesis," 337.

[20] Augustine, "Reply to Faustus the Manichaean," bk. 12, chap. 6, in *Nicene and Post-Nicene Fathers,* 1st ser., vol. 4, ed. Philip Schaff (Peabody, MA: 1887), 274.

[21] Augustine, "On Christian Doctrine," bk. 1, chap. 36, in *Nicene and Post-Nicene Fathers,* 1st ser., vol. 2, ed. Philip Schaff; trans. J. F. Shaw (Buffalo: Christian Literature, 1887), 533.

This means, of course, that interpretation of the Bible is not undertaken by a detached, "objective" observer, but by one who is committed already to its truth, overall shape, and moral force.

Like others before him, Augustine detected both literal and figurative levels of meaning in the biblical texts (which he sometimes referred to as "letter" and "spirit"):

> We should not take in the literal sense any figurative phrase which in the proper meaning of its words would produce only nonsense, but should consider what else it signifies, nourishing the inner man by our spiritual intelligence, since being carnally-minded is death, while to be spiritually-minded is life and peace. If, for instance, a man were to take in a literal and carnal sense much that is written in the Song of Solomon, he would minister not to the fruit of a luminous charity, but to the feeling of a libidinous desire.[22]

But Augustine went beyond his predecessors in articulating the theoretical point that humans, whose capacity for mental images and rationality is "grounded in the divine Logos,"[23] use words as communicative *signifiers*: "No one uses words except as signs of something else," he wrote, "and hence may be understood what I call signs: those things, to wit, which are used to indicate something else."[24]

This insight, as obvious as it might now seem, has proven to be important in the study of language. Twentieth-century linguist Karl Bühler insisted that "language phenomena are significative through and through."[25]

For Augustine, word-signs may operate with direct or figurative signification. Some of the significations in Scripture are obscure:

> But hasty and careless readers are led astray by many and manifold obscurities and ambiguities, substituting one meaning for another; and in some places they cannot hit upon even a fair interpretation. Some of the expressions are so obscure as to shroud the meaning in the thickest

---

[22] Augustine, "On the Spirit and the Letter," chap. 6, in *Nicene and Post-Nicene Fathers*, 1st ser., vol. 5, ed. Philip Schaff; trans. Peter Holmes and Robert Ernest Wallis, rev. Benjamin B. Warfield (Buffalo: Christian Literature, 1887), 85.

[23] Jens Zimmermann, *Recovering Theological Hermeneutics: An Incarnational-Trinitarian Theory of Interpretation* (Grand Rapids: Baker Academic, 2004), 167.

[24] Augustine, "On Christian Doctrine," bk. 1, chap. 2, 523.

[25] Karl Bühler, *Theory of Language: The Representational Function of Language*, trans. Donald Fraser Goodwin (Amsterdam: John Benjamins, 2011 [German original 1934/1982]).

darkness. And I do not doubt that all this was divinely arranged for the purpose of subduing pride by toil, and of preventing a feeling of satiety in the intellect, which generally holds in small esteem what is discovered without difficulty.[26]

But the benefit of figurative language is that it can elicit a more fervent response than plain language, even though it has a greater danger of being misunderstood:

Does the hearer learn anything more than when he listens to the same thought expressed in plain language, without the help of this figure? And yet, I don't know why, I feel greater pleasure. . . .
Accordingly the Holy Spirit has, with admirable wisdom and care for our welfare, so arranged the Holy Scriptures as by the plainer passages to satisfy our hunger, and by the more obscure to stimulate our appetite.[27]

Either way, whether directly or figuratively, words refer to other realities. This is an important observation, because this link between words and realities comes into question later in the history of hermeneutics. Stanley Porter and Jason Robinson sum up French philosopher Jacques Derrida's hesitation about the link between word-signs and realities: "He sees all things as texts and everything we are conscious of as a play of differences always deferring, never fully present, and never reaching closure. . . . Life can be read the same way one reads a text, i.e. as signifiers referring to other signifiers for meaning without any ideal signified."[28]

Augustine was far more optimistic. But note that he did not require that words refer directly to *external* realities; rather, they express, and conjure, "inner speech" regarding those external realities. Jean Grondin, a professor of philosophy, observed, "In conceiving the word as a process whereby spirit, fully present in the Word

> *I find author Alexander S. Jensen's illustration helpful: "Language does not refer to things, but to our mental images of things. So when I tell a funny story that happened to me with a horse, then this story, this word, to use Augustine's terminology, does not refer to the event itself, but to my mental image of the event. So the hearer does not gain knowledge about the event itself, but of my mental image of it. He or she will form a mental image, which is recovered from my narrative."**
>
> *Alexander S. Jensen, *Theological Hermeneutics* (London: SCM Press, 2007), 41.

---

[26] Augustine, "On Christian Doctrine," bk. 2, chapter 6, 537.
[27] Ibid.
[28] Stanley E. Porter and Jason C. Robinson, *Hermeneutics: An Introduction to Interpretive Theory* (Grand Rapids: Eerdmans, 2011), 204.

and yet referring to Another, is incarnated, Augustine reveals that hermeneutics is universally bound to language."[29]

When Augustine read the Bible, he took the mental images conjured by Scripture to be true, affirmed as they are by God's Spirit—even if he was not certain of the precise intentions of the human author.

At the same time as this interest in what is at stake in human language and interpretation, Augustine advocated and practiced a consciousness of one's own finitude, and a correlative concern for continued listening, in dependence on God. In Augustine's *Confessions* we see a disciple's provisional grasp of the Scriptures, expressed in deeply humble conversation with the God of the Scriptures. This image cannot help but remind of Plato's vision of dialectic, but with the added dimension that the text's divine Author remains living and reachable—without being exhaustible or containable. The voice of the divine Author is heard in the Scriptures, and the devoted hearer expects that his meditative reflection on the Scriptures will be heard and helped by God: "Long time have I burned to meditate in Thy law, and in it to confess to Thee my knowledge and ignorance, the beginning of Thine enlightening, and the remains of my darkness, until infirmity be swallowed up by strength."[30]

Of course, while Plato gave critical definition to this sort of dialogical engagement, the practice itself has a strong heritage in the Hebrew Bible, where psalmists spoke out their meditation on scriptural themes to the Lord. Prof. Jens Zimmermann, who specializes in hermeneutics, tells us that "premodern interpretation at its best remained faithful to the Hebraic concept of dialoguing with the Divine through the text."[31]

Chrysostom

John Chrysostom (349–407), while giving less explicit attention to the conditions or mechanics of language or interpretation, exemplified the way the dialogical engagement Zimmermann described could be practiced not only within the relationship between the reader and the divine Author, but also between the reader and the human author. Chrysostom dialogued with the (presumed) authors of the text, inquisitively seeking answers from the text itself:

---

[29] Jean Grondin, *Introduction to Philosophical Hermeneutics*, Yale Studies in Hermeneutics ed., trans. Joel Weinsheimer (New Haven, CT, and London: Yale University Press, 1997), 33.

[30] Augustine, *Confessions*, bk. 11, chap. 1, in Philip Schaff, ed., *Nicene and Post-Nicene Fathers*, 1st ser., vol. 1 (Buffalo: Christian Literature, 1886), 163.

[31] Zimmermann, *Recovering Theological Hermeneutics*, 29.

> What do you mean, Moses? Is there any comparison at all between the true God and false gods? Moses would reply: "I did not say this to make a comparison . . ."[32]

> What do you mean, David? Is this a strange marvel? No, he said. For this was not the only thing he saw.[33]

> What do you mean, Paul? Am I to be subject to God in the same way the clay is to the potter? Yes, Paul says.[34]

Margaret Mitchell, dean of the University of Chicago Divinity School, has commented at length on the relationship between Chrysostom and Paul, and offered the following translation of a key reflection by Chrysostom: "Continually when I hear the letters of the blessed Paul read . . . I rejoice in the pleasure of that spiritual trumpet, and am roused to attention and warmed with desire because I recognize the voice I love . . . , and seem to imagine him all but present and see him conversing with me."[35]

This sort of practice of dialogical understanding of texts would later be given rigorous universalizing defense, as we will especially see when we come to the philosophical hermeneutics of Gadamer.

Bede and Aquinas

Following from the patristic interpreters before them, interpreters from the Middle Ages generally understood the key theme of Scripture to be the person of Jesus Christ. They believed that every Scripture is God-breathed and useful for teaching, correcting, rebuking and training in righteousness (2 Tim 3:16-17). Thus, in settings of ministry application, they sometimes sought ways of detecting didactic significance beyond the surface of Scripture—whether Old Testament, Gospel, narrative, or parable. However, this figurative gospel interpretation was

---

[32] John Chrysostom, "Against the Jews," 5.3.3, http://www.tertullian.org/fathers/chrysostom_adversus_judaeos_05_homily5.htm; accessed April 29, 2017.

[33] Ibid., 7.2.5, http://www.tertullian.org/fathers/chrysostom_adversus_judaeos_07_homily7.htm; accessed April 29, 2017.

[34] John Chrysostom, "On the Incomprehensible Nature of God," 2.35 in *The Fathers of the Church: St. John Chrysostom on the Incomprehensible Nature of God*, trans. Paul W. Harkins (Washington, DC: Catholic University of America Press, 1984), 85.

[35] Margaret M. Mitchell, *The Heavenly Trumpet: John Chrysostom and the Art of Pauline Interpretation* (Louisville: Westminster John Knox Press, 2002), 37.

not necessarily thought to override the surface meaning of the passage—multiple levels were able to be heard.

Bede

The Venerable Bede (673–735) provides a good example of this general interpretive impulse. He is frequently thought of as one who got carried away with allegory. Here he is reflecting on Matt 2:13–23:

> Now figuratively speaking, Rachel, which means "sheep" or "seeing God," stands for the Church, who with her whole attention keeps watch so that she may deserve to see God. And she is that hundredth sheep whom the good shepherd goes out to seek on earth, having left behind the ninety-nine sheep of the angelic virtues in heaven; and when he finds her, he puts her on his shoulders and carries her back to the flock. However, according to the literal sense, the question arises how it may be said that Rachel bewailed her children, since the tribe of Judah, which contained Bethlehem, sprang not from Rachel, but from her sister Leah.[36]

Note that Bede's allegorical/figurative reading is only *one* "sense" of meaning that he discerned in the text; it does not drown out a "literal sense." Furthermore, his figurative reading is constrained by the gospel of the Good Shepherd.

Bede elsewhere reflected on what happens hermeneutically when Christians read the Old Testament: they are able to gain nourishment by drinking it in as "water"; but this water is transformed into "wine" when they perceive its full Christological significance:

> If upon hearing of the horrible devastation of this disaster [of the flood in the time of Noah], and the marvelous deliverance of a few, one begins to live more faultlessly, desiring to be delivered with the elect and fearing to be exterminated with the condemned, one unquestionably has received a [jar] of water by which one may be cleansed or refreshed. But one may begin to see at a more profound level, and come to an understanding of the ark as the Church; of Noah as Christ; of the water which washed away sinners as the waters of baptism, which washes away sins. . . . [One who has this deeper understanding] unquestionably marvels at wine

---

[36] Homily 1.10 in Bede the Venerable, *Homilies on the Gospels*, 97–98 (see preface, n. 1).

made from water, for in the history of the ancient deeds he contemplates his own cleansing, sanctification, and justification being foretold.[37]

Aquinas

Thomas Aquinas (1225–1274) was likewise explicit and unapologetic about approaching the Bible with a theologically informed pre-understanding. He regarded the New Testament letters as having a divinely ordained arrangement that informs people of God's way of salvation, such that Hebrews points to Christ, Romans points to grace, 1 Corinthians points to the means of grace in the sacraments, 2 Corinthians discusses the ministers of the sacraments, and so on.

His actual analysis of each New Testament letter, however, was not constantly or forcibly directed by his pre-understanding of the letter's overall divine function. He seemed content to comment on the varied issues of each letter as they come up, without repeatedly tying every strand to a singular theme or function. He customarily commented on structure, meanings of words, relation to other parts of Scripture, and relation to church practice. He also offered occasional speculation about historical setting. For example, in his Commentary on 1 Corinthians, he pondered whether Chloe (1:11) might come from a villa under the jurisdiction of the Corinthians, or be the matron of a household in which believers met (11:24).[38]

Aquinas stepped back to reflect on the relationship between theology and the Bible at the beginning of his magnum opus, *Summa Theologiae*. His major proposal was that sacred Scripture and sacred doctrine are united. At the outset of his investigation, he cited 2 Tim 3:16, insisting that God's inspired revelation is necessary for humans. But it is not studied in a way that is separable *before* philosophical theologizing; rather, it is understood *with* "philosophical science" (I,q,1,a.1). For Aquinas, the goal of any sort of interpretation was *penetrative understanding*. Similarly to Augustine, this entails coming to understand the thought of the author. It also involves seeing the text's relationship to other truths of Scripture and theology.

Aquinas considered the objection that the "low" and "corporeal" figures of human speech are not fit for the delivery of clear divine truth. His response was

---

[37] Homily 1.14 in Bede the Venerable, *Homilies on the Gospels*, 140.
[38] See Thomas Aquinas, *Super I Epistolam B. Pauli ad Corinthios lectura* (Commentary on the First Epistle to the Corinthians), trans. Fabian Archer, chaps. 1–2, par. 24, http://dhspriory.org/thomas/SS1Cor.htm#12.

essentially that God is able to communicate analogically—that is, by analogy with corporeal things—thereby accommodating to human understanding. He wrote,

> It is befitting Holy Writ to put forward divine and spiritual truths by means of comparisons with material things. For God provides for everything according to the capacity of its nature. Now it is natural to man to attain to intellectual truths through sensible objects, because all our knowledge originates from sense. Hence in Holy Writ, spiritual truths are fittingly taught under the likeness of material things. . . . in order that thereby even the simple who are unable by themselves to grasp intellectual things may be able to understand it.[39]

As in Augustine's work *On Christian Doctrine*, Aquinas considered that while there are parts of Scripture that are unclear due to their figurative nature, these are countered by other parts of Scripture that speak plainly: "Hence those things that are taught metaphorically in one part of Scripture, in other parts are taught more openly."[40]

Also like Augustine, Aquinas considered that words may offer a literal signification or a figurative signification. For Aquinas, as for many before him, *all* Scripture may be read according to both the "literal" sense, and the further "spiritual" sense. Note, though, that the spiritual sense depends on, rather than replaces, the literal sense (I,q.1,a.10). The spiritual sense may in practice be an allegorical, tropological (moral), or anagogical (eschatological) interpretation. Again, like Augustine, Aquinas was content to defer certainty about a singular intended meaning.

Beatrice of Nazareth and Angela of Foligno

At the same time that the Bible and its interpretation were being discussed in academic and clerical settings, interpretation of the Bible continued being practiced in lay ecclesial settings and religious orders. Two figures worth mentioning in this regard are Beatrice of Nazareth and Angela of Foligno.

---

[39] Thomas Aquinas, *The Summa Theologiae of Saint Thomas Aquinas*, Latin-English ed., vol. 1, *Prima Pars*, Q.1–64 (Scotts Valley, CA: NovAntiqua, 2008), I.q.1,a.9; 14–15.
[40] Ibid., 15.

Beatrice of Nazareth

In *The Seven Ways of Holy Love*, Beatrice of Nazareth (1200–1268) conducted what might be called a mystical meditation on the nature of love. She explored the varied, ascending experiences of the human soul in seeking to love and in perceiving the love of God. This work is steeped in certain themes of Scripture, and both cites and evokes numerous phrases or passages of Scripture, rather than being a methodical exposition of a particular section of Scripture.

Angela of Foligno

Angela of Foligno (1248–1309) was canonized in the twenty-first century by Pope Francis. Francis's predecessor, Benedict XVI, remembered Angela as "a great medieval mystic," who came to repentance after terrible personal tragedy, and eventually came to celebrate the love of God as focused in the crucified Christ.[41] This focus directed her exposition of Scripture, providing a provisional sense of the burden of the Bible for its hearers. As Darleen Pryds, of the Franciscan School of Theology, has pointed out, "Her graphic descriptions [of the cross] illustrate the kind of theological and spiritual study that she supported and the form of theological and spiritual teaching that she offered. Hers was a visceral form of study and understanding of Scripture. In turn, this is the kind of active engagement she encouraged in her followers, who included both laity and clergy."[42]

Conclusion

The survey in this chapter has covered an abundance of history. Before we continue on with history in the next chapter, it is worth briefly drawing attention to some themes that have emerged. First, it is evident that the figures surveyed believed that interpretation requires work, because it involves seeking a connection between genuine *others*. Even if the meaning is thought to be plain, it still needs to be discerned by carefully informed hearers or readers. Second—and linked to the first issue—it is

> **BIG IDEA**
>
> The early history of hermeneutics suggests that interpretation of texts involves a multifaceted encounter of others.

---

[41] Benedict XVI, "Blessed Angela of Foligno," October 13, 2010, on the Vatican's website, https://w2.vatican.va/content/benedict-xvi/en/audiences/2010/documents/hf_ben-xvi_aud_20101013.html.

[42] Darleen Pryds, "Angela of Foligno," in Marion Ann Taylor, ed., *Handbook of Women Biblical Interpreters: A Historical and Biographical Guide* (Grand Rapids: Baker Academic, 2012), 38.

important to Christian interpreters that their reading of Scripture be informed by certain theological truths, such as the centrality of Christ (or his cross), or the need to show love for God and neighbor. Third, there was a definite interest in the intentions of the author by those we have surveyed, but they also seemed reasonably comfortable with the possibility of discerning multiple meanings or multiple layers of meaning.

Questions for Discussion

1. What does it mean that a text is "other" than ourselves? In what ways will this affect interpretation?

2. Is it fair for Christian interpreters to bring theological truths or assumptions to the text? Will this help or hinder their ability to hear the biblical texts?

3. If it is appropriate to bring theological assumptions to one's reading of Scripture, which assumptions should be brought? How do you evaluate those that have come out so far in our overview—the centrality of Christ and the need for love of God and neighbor?

4. Can a text have more than one meaning, or more than one layer of meaning? Can you think of any examples of passages in which this might be the case? Can you think of any examples of passages for which there is no room for multiple levels or meanings?

5. Which historical figures from this chapter do you resonate with? Why? Are there any that you find unpersuasive?

For Further Reading

Augustine. "On Christian Doctrine." Bk. 1. Chap. 36. In *Nicene and Post-Nicene Fathers*, 1st ser, vol. 2, edited by Philip Schaff; translated by J. F. Shaw. Buffalo: Christian Literature, 1887.

3

HISTORY OF HERMENEUTICS, PART 2: LUTHER TO PRESENT DAY

In this chapter we will continue to listen to the voices of theorists and practitioners of interpretation.

Luther and Calvin

Luther

Martin Luther (1483–1546) strenuously insisted on a plain reading of the biblical texts—a reading that is just as accessible to ordinary believers as to the priesthood. He complained that nothing is "more miserable than uncertainty"[1] and railed against what he saw as Roman muddying of the clear waters of Scripture.[2]

However, Luther's "plain reading" of biblical texts does depend upon a number of interpretive principles, especially regarding the ultimacy of Christ and the priority of "Gospel" over "Law":

> Now the gospels and epistles of the apostles were written for this very purpose. They want themselves to be our guides, to direct us to the

---

[1] Martin Luther, *On the Bondage of the Will*, in J. J. Pelikan, H. C. Oswald, & H. T. Lehmann (eds.), *Luther's Works, vol. 33: Career of the Reformer III* (Philadelphia: Fortress Press, 1999), 22.
[2] This does not mean that Luther thought full interpretative closure was simple—or even possible: "We must ever remain scholars here; we cannot sound the depth of one single verse in Scripture; we get hold but of the A B C, and that imperfectly." Martin Luther, *Tabletalk*, trans. William Hazlitt (Fearn, UK: Christian Focus, 2003), 96.

writings of the prophets and of Moses in the Old Testament so that we might there read and see for ourselves how Christ is wrapped in swaddling cloths and laid in the manger [Luke 2:7], that is, how he is comprehended [*Vorfassett*] in the writings of the prophets. It is there that people like us should read and study, drill ourselves, and see what Christ is, for what purpose he has been given, how he was promised, and how all Scripture tends toward him.[3]

The knowledge of this topic, the distinction between the Law and the Gospel, is necessary to the highest degree; for it contains a summary of all Christian doctrine.[4]

At times, it seems that these principles require a repudiation of what otherwise might seem to be the "plain reading" of a passage. British theologian Susan Gillingham commented on Luther's reading of Psalm 1:

Put quite simply, Psalm 1 proved a challenge for how Luther worked out his antithetical theology of "Law" and "Gospel." The key problem was how a Christian could "delight in the Law": for this Law brought about the self-righteousness of the Jews which led to their rejection of Christ, and similarly encouraged the works-righteousness of the Roman Church, which resulted in both the suppression of the laity and indeed of the true voice of Scripture itself.[5]

On Luther's reading of the psalm, the wicked sinners of verse 1 are the Jews (and subsequently the leaders of the Roman Catholic Church), who "turn the Law of God into human tradition or human tradition into the Law of God."[6] Thus, although one might have thought that a "plain reading" would see the believer as delighting in keeping God's law, Luther's hermeneutical pre-understanding was that God's Word promotes the gospel of God's Son, a gospel that is opposed to the demand for law keeping. Thus, on a Christian reading, the truly blessed man of Psalm 1 is Christ himself, who graciously shares his blessing with those who

---

[3] Martin Luther, *Luther's Works*, vol. 35, *Word and Sacrament I*, ed. J. J. Pelikan, H. C. Oswald, and H. T. Lehmann (Philadelphia: Fortress Press, 1999), 122.
[4] Martin Luther, *Luther's Works*, vol. 26, *Lectures on Galatians, 1535, Chapters 1–4*, ed. J. J. Pelikan, H. C. Oswald, and H. T. Lehmann (Saint Louis: Concordia, 1999), 117.
[5] Susan Gillingham, *A Journey of Two Psalms: The Reception of Psalms 1 and 2 in Jewish and Christian Tradition* (Oxford: Oxford University Press, 2013), 118.
[6] Cited in ibid., 119.

have faith in him. Their delight in the law is really a delight in the One who has fulfilled the law. Gillingham summarized the continued trajectory of Luther's approach in Alesius (1500–65): "The psalm speaks about how the Law brings about judgement to those who are proud in their own achievements and blessedness to those who trust only in God's goodness, knowing they can never attain the Law's demands but only accept the mercy and forgiveness offered by the Gospel of Christ. The 'delight in the Law' is thus the result of being blessed, not the condition for it."[7]

Kenneth Hagen, an expert on the Reformation at Marquette University, commented:

> As a biblical interpreter Luther remained firmly rooted in the medieval approach to the text, the so-called "spiritual reading" (*lectio divina*). . . .
> Like his patristic and medieval predecessors . . . Luther saw Christ as the heart of the Psalter.[8]

Calvin

John Calvin's (1509–1564) reading of Psalm 1 might seem to be plainer than that of Luther or his heirs: "The meaning of the Psalmist . . . is, that it shall be always well with God's devout servants, whose constant endeavour it is to make progress in the study of his law."[9]

Calvin elsewhere pleaded, "Let us know, then, that the true meaning of Scripture is the natural and obvious meaning; and let us embrace and abide by it resolutely. Let us not only neglect as doubtful, but boldly set aside as deadly corruptions, those pretended expositions, which lead us away from the natural meaning."[10]

Gillingham has pointed out that "Calvin's systematic approach to reading the psalms would usually be to look first at the meaning of the psalms in the life of David, then in the life of Christ, then in the life of the Church."[11]

---

[7] Ibid., 122.

[8] Kenneth Hagen, "*Omnis homo mendax*: Luther on Psalm 116," in Richard A. Muller and John L. Thompson, eds., *Biblical Interpretation in the Era of the Reformation* (Grand Rapids: Eerdmans, 1996), 85–86.

[9] John Calvin, *Commentary upon the Book of Psalms*, trans. James Anderson, Calvin's Commentaries (Grand Rapids: Baker, 1979 [original 1571]), 4:1–2.

[10] John Calvin, *The Epistles of Paul*, cited in Cornelis Van Dam, "Interpreting Historical Narrative: Truth Claim, Truth Value, and Historicity," in Mees te Velde and Gerhard H. Visscher, eds., *Correctly Handling the Word of Truth* (Eugene, OR: Wipf & Stock, 2014), 95.

[11] Gillingham, *A Journey of Two Psalms*, 123n99.

Thus, while Luther's hermeneutical principle of an antithesis between law and gospel in both Old and New Testaments[12] led him to offer a more complex Christocentric reading of Psalm 1, Calvin's rather different hermeneutical pre-understanding, that the Old Testament is *preparation* for the gospel, led him to read the psalm in a way that defers figurative meanings:

> Calvin was most critical of the allegorical method, which . . . was widely used by commentators in both the western and eastern churches (and especially used by both Erasmus and Luther) in their search for hidden (Christian) meanings in these psalms. Instead Calvin preferred a typological reading, applying, first, a "historical" David-centred way of reading each psalm and then, secondly, a "theological" Christ-centred way of reading it. This of course allowed a greater appreciation of the Jewish roots of the psalms and distanced Calvin from reformers such as Erasmus and Luther.[13]

Note, though, that such a reading is no less "hermeneutical" or theologically influenced than that of Luther. Calvin's sense of the "natural" meaning of Scripture is guided by the theological conviction that the Old Testament is oriented to Christ through typological foreshadowing and deferral of clear disclosure of the gospel itself: "I do indeed acknowledge that these things relate to the kingdom of Christ, and that they were at length fulfilled as soon as the Gospel began to be preached; but it does not therefore follow that the Prophet did not, at the same time, keep his eye upon that period which preceded the coming of Christ."[14]

When Calvin's plea for the natural and obvious sense of Scripture was taken up in the present day by Canadian Old Testament scholar Cornelis Van Dam, he urged, "We should speak of understanding the obvious meaning of the text."[15] But it was just as obvious to Luther that Psalm 1 is about Christ as it was to Calvin

---

[12] James Samuel Preus, whose expertise was in Old Testament hermeneutics, commented on the relationship between Old and New Testaments, and law and gospel in Luther's thought: "The 'divide' no longer lies between the testaments, but begins to appear as a distinction grounded in the Old Testament itself—between its law and its promise, between 'two testaments' found there, between the 'law of Moses' and the 'law of the Lord.'" James Samuel Preus, *From Shadow to Promise: Old Testament Interpretation from Augustine to the Young Luther* (Cambridge, MA: Harvard University Press, 1969), 200.

[13] Gillingham, *A Journey of Two Psalms*, 128.

[14] John Calvin, *Commentary on Isaiah*, 54:2, Calvin's Commentaries, vol. 8, repr. (Grand Rapids: Baker, 1979), 135 of sub-volume 4.

[15] Van Dam, "Interpreting Historical Narrative," 95.

that Psalm 1 is about the ideal believer. This is not to say that the concept of a plain or obvious meaning of Scripture is irretrievable, but that proponents of such a view could probably be more precise by pleading for readings of Scripture that are "plain" and "obvious" *to readers who have been shaped by an appropriate theological assessment of what Scripture is doing as divine address about Christ.*

It should not be thought, however, that approaching the scriptural text with theological assumptions means giving no consideration to historical concerns. On the contrary, the "return to the sources" characteristic of the Renaissance is very apparent in the key Reformers. Introducing his commentary on Galatians, Calvin stated, "One who forms his views of the subject from the Commentaries of Origen and Jerome, will be astonished that Paul should take so deep an interest in external rites; but whoever goes to the fountain will acknowledge that there was abundant reason for all this sharpness of reproof."[16]

The emphasis by both Luther and Calvin on the Scriptures as a fountain accessible to those outside of the priesthood has been very influential on subsequent hermeneutical discussions. Calvin's downplaying of the figurative, and his ridicule of the allegorical method, no doubt contributed to the growing emphasis in Protestant interpretation on the conditions of the emergence of scriptural texts as products of historically located human authors.

Schleiermacher and Dilthey

Schleiermacher

Friedrich Schleiermacher (1768–1834) is considered one of the fathers of modern hermeneutics. He carried forward a movement that had been developing in the seventeenth century. This movement made explicit the universal character of hermeneutics by characterizing it as a consideration of what is at stake in human understanding in general. German philosopher Martin Heidegger wrote of this period: "Hermeneutics is now no longer interpretation itself, but a doctrine about the conditions, the objects, the means, and the communication and practical application of interpretation."[17]

Historian Wilhelm Dilthey (1833–1911) presented the common, though disputed, understanding that Schleiermacher brought about a new universalization

---

[16] John Calvin, *Commentaries on the Epistles of Paul to the Galatians and Ephesians*, trans. William Pringle, repr. (Grand Rapids: Baker, 1979), 15.

[17] Martin Heidegger, *Ontology—The Hermeneutics of Facticity*, trans. John van Buren (Bloomington: Indiana University Press, 1999 [original 1988]), 10.

of the discipline, departing from the regionalized study of interpretive rules, and coming to the consideration of universal conditions of human understanding:

> Until [Schleiermacher] then, hermeneutics had at best been an edifice of rules, the parts of which—the individual rules—were held together by the aim to achieve a valid interpretation. . . . Now Schleiermacher went behind these rules to the analysis of understanding, i.e. to the comprehension of the purposive act itself and from this comprehension he deduced the possibility of valid interpretation, its aids, limits and rules.[18]

In considering the conditions of human understanding, Schleiermacher appropriated the idea of the "hermeneutical circle," which we discussed earlier: "Complete knowledge is always in this apparent circle, that each particular can only be understood via the general, of which it is a part, and vice versa. And every piece of knowledge is only scientific if it is formed in this way."[19]

This image has become a stable feature in discussion of hermeneutics. It is sometimes misunderstood, however. The hermeneutical circle is not simply a circular movement between the modern reader and the ancient text. As we saw in chapter 1, it is rather a refining movement between a general sense and a more particular analysis. It begins with "pre-understanding" (*vorverstehen*) and continually proceeds toward a refined understanding.

The hermeneutical goal for Schleiermacher was to enter, via a grammatical and artful study of the text, into the author's experience. While the emphasis on *experience* is typical of the Romantic movement, with which Schleiermacher is often associated, the emphases on *grammatical analysis* and the *author* are typical

---

[18] W. Dilthey, "The Development of Hermeneutics," in H. P. Rickman, ed., *Dilthey: Selected Writings* (Cambridge University Press, 1976 [original 1900]), 256. Note that the special place of Schleiermacher in "universalizing" hermeneutics was qualified by Jean Grondin, who wrote, "These general theories of interpretation [during the seventeenth century] broke through the limits of the regional hermeneutics—that is, the manuals—that were specifically designed to help in elucidating Scripture or classical authors. Consequently, the development of the first supraregional art of interpretation cannot be justly ascribed to Schleiermacher." Jean Grondin, *Introduction to Philosophical Hermeneutics*, Yale Studies in Hermeneutics (New Haven, CT: Yale University Press, 1994), 4. Grondin assigned certain sorts of universality to precritical hermeneutics. Zimmermann went further, insisting that the "communion with God" aimed at in precritical Christian hermeneutics was emphatically universal: "Theological interpretation did indeed formulate rules for biblical interpretation, but it did so in the context of worldview thinking." Zimmermann, *Recovering Theological Hermeneutics*, 18 (see chap. 2, n. 24).

[19] Schleiermacher, "Hermeneutics and Criticism," 24 (see chap. 1, n. 10). Cf. 27, where Schleiermacher offers as a methodological rule the need to begin with a "general overview."

of the historical-critical impulses that thrived after the Reformation, especially with the Enlightenment. Consider the stress on the author's language in Schleiermacher's consideration of the grammatical side of interpretation (and note the similarity to Augustine's conception of communication): "Laws of language and content of their parts must be given. What is being sought is the same thing in the [inner] thought which the utterer wanted to express."[20]

Further, consider the importance of the author's intentions in the "technical ['artful'] side of interpretation": "The point of the task is to understand the particular part of a coherent utterance as belonging in the specific sequence of thoughts of the writer."[21]

The "thoughts of the writer" have a disputed place in hermeneutical reflection. In recent discussion there is more interest in acknowledging *textual directedness* than in attempting to re-create an uncertain authorial experience.[22]

Dilthey

Dilthey, who devoted much of his writing career to the work of Schleiermacher, is remembered as continuing to explicitly universalize the scope of hermeneutics and emphasizing the historical conditioning of human understanding. He insisted that because the human sciences (which he controversially distinguished from the natural sciences) depend on "interpretive knowledge,"[23] they must be grounded in a general theory of human interpretation:

> [The main task of hermeneutics] is to counteract the constant irruption of romantic whim and sceptical subjectivity into the realm of history by laying the historical foundations of valid interpretation on which all certainty in history rests. Absorbed into the context of the epistemology, logic and methodology of the human studies[,] the theory of interpretation becomes a vital link between philosophy and the historical disciplines, an essential part of the foundations of the studies of man.[24]

---

[20] Schleiermacher, "General Hermeneutics," in *Hermeneutics and Criticism*, 233 (see chap. 1, n. 10).

[21] Schleiermacher, "General Hermeneutics," 254.

[22] Note that on Thiselton's reading (*Hermeneutics*, chap. 8; see my chap. 1, n. 2), Schleiermacher himself is best characterized as interested in entextualized directedness, more than imagined authorial psychology.

[23] This is Grondin's phrase: *Introduction to Philosophical Hermeneutics*, 6.

[24] Dilthey, "The Development of Hermeneutics," 260.

Thiselton emphasized Dilthey's concern for historical foundations: "Hermeneutics in the more recent sense of the term begins with the recognition that historical conditioning is two-sided: *the modern interpreter, no less than the text, stands in a given historical context and tradition*."[25]

New Criticism and New Hermeneutic

New Criticism and Its Critics

It is worth noting that the emphasis of Schleiermacher, Dilthey, and many others on the context and intentionality of the author behind the text gave way in the midtwentieth century to doubts about the accessibility of the author behind the text. This echoes Plato's caution that written texts can no longer be defended or clarified by their authors, but take on a life of their own. This perspective led for a while, in literary studies, to a strong focus on the text itself—particularly for poetic or narrative texts.

Literary structuralism emerged with the hope of providing a more objective approach to determining a text's internal meaning. In relation to narrative, one application was the attempt to determine the "deep structure" of a story, identifying key roles, such as "hero" or "villain," and key functions, such as "conflict" and "reconciliation." It is this deep structure that was said to reveal the meaning of the text.

This focus on texts abstracted from their historical locatedness was rather short-lived and gave way to new interest in the place of the reader. Indeed, it is more than possible that the very identification of heroes and villains in a text might communicate more about the reader than about the text.

Reader-response theory emerged in part as a response to Schleiermacher's overemphasis on the author and the overconfidence of New Criticism in the text. The most famous representative of this movement would perhaps be Stanley Fish (1938–). This movement recognizes that as

As an example, imagine I come home with a friend to find a note written by my wife, saying, "The girls are in detention." This is a rather open text: Which girls? Detention where? My friend might interpret the note to mean that my daughters are being kept late after school. But as a relationally primed reader, I would interpret it to mean that our three chickens were in the separate coop where they are put if they become broody. This involves a lot of reading between the lines on my part, but this is precisely what interpretation involves.

---

[25] Thiselton, *The Two Horizons*, 11 (see chap. 1, n. 13); emphasis in original.

much as author and text contribute, understanding will not occur without the contribution of the reader.

Different readers will bring different assumptions and commitments to the text, resulting in different interpretations. In some situations, such as a poetry reading, such variety may be positively celebrated. In other settings, such as interpreting the instructions on an escape hatch, it might be disastrous.

New Hermeneutic

Ernst Fuchs (1903–1983) and Gerhard Ebeling (1912–2001), two students of Lutheran theologian Rudolf Bultmann, are associated with the "New Hermeneutic," which dealt with the problem of history somewhat differently than the New Criticism. Whereas in literary studies, attention was being directed away from the prehistory of literary texts and toward the text itself or its readers, the New Hermeneutic sought to restore interest in the history behind the text, but to separate this historical examination sharply from the reader's discernment of its existential meaning.

This takes seriously the need for an actualization of the text in the life of the reader, operating from a conviction that God confronts the individual in the Scriptures; but this actualizing divine encounter appears to happen despite the contingencies of the text, rather than in continuity with them. In this respect it represents a stream of hermeneutical reflection somewhat at odds with the positive appropriation of locatedness seen in Schleiermacher.

Heidegger, Gadamer, Ricoeur, and Thiselton

At the same time that these discussions were taking place in the fields of literary and biblical studies, further philosophical discussion on *hermeneutics as the study of human understanding* was also taking place, in the wake of Schleiermacher and Dilthey.

Heidegger

Philosopher Martin Heidegger (1889–1976), who was influential for those of the "New Hermeneutic," was also important for those who were to build more positively on Schleiermacher's hermeneutical legacy. Heidegger sought to reconfigure philosophy in a way that did justice to the locatedness of the subject. He emphasized that there can be no "being" apart from "being there" (*dasein*)—in a particular location of place and time: "Time must be brought to light and genuinely grasped as the horizon of every understanding and interpretation of being," he wrote.[26]

Heidegger was interested in the contextualized self-awareness that is fundamental to acts of communication: "This relationship with its object which . . . hermeneutics enjoys on the level of *being* makes the inception, execution, and appropriation of hermeneutics prior ontologically and factico-temporally to all accomplishments in the sciences."[27]

Heidegger sought,[28] with hermeneutics, to prompt a "radical wakefulness" for the located self.

Gadamer

Drawing on the philosophy of Heidegger, as well as the work of Schleiermacher and Dilthey, Hans-Georg Gadamer (1900–2002) presented the separated (embodied) locatedness of the textual horizon and the interpreter's horizon not as a problem to be overcome as much as an examinable span across which communication is necessarily mediated:

> Time is no longer primarily a gulf to be bridged, because it separates, but it is actually the supportive ground of process in which the present is rooted. Hence temporal distance is not something that must be overcome . . . In fact the important thing is to recognise the distance in time as a positive and productive possibility of understanding. It is not a yawning abyss, but is filled with the continuity of customs and traditions, in the light of which all that is handed down presents itself to us.[29]

Gadamer employed the image of conversation to describe the traversing of this stretch between the horizon of the text and the horizon of the reader: "In itself, all speaking has the character of 'speaking with someone' and, as such, intends that what it speaks about should be understood as the kind of thing that the speech makes it visible as. Even where, in fact, no one else is present to hear my words, the assumption inherent in what I say is still that it is understandable

---

[26] Martin Heidegger, *Being and Time*, trans. Joan Stambaugh (Albany: State University of New York Press, 2010 [original 1953]), 17.

[27] Heidegger, *Ontology*, 12; emphasis added.

[28] It might be more precise to say the early Heidegger, given that his *Ontology* preceded his *Being and Time* and evidences an early interest in hermeneutics itself.

[29] Hans-Georg Gadamer, *Truth and Method*, trans. Joel Weinsheimer and Donald G. Marshall. 2nd rev. ed. (London: Continuum, 2004). (Translation of *Wahrheit und Methode: Grundzüge einer philosophischen Hermeneutik*. 2nd ed. [Tubingen: J. C. B. Mohr, 1960], 264–65.)

by others."[30] This is appropriate, because human thought and understanding at its most basic levels is already conversational, or "dialogical":

> Plato calls thought the inner dialogue of the soul with itself. Here the structure of the matter becomes completely apparent. It is called dialogue because it consists of question and answer, since one asks oneself just as one asks another, and says something to oneself just like saying it to someone else. Augustine long ago referred to this way of talking to oneself. Everyone is, as it were, a conversation with themselves. Even those in conversation with others must remain in conversation with themselves insofar as they continue to think.
>
> Language finds its paradigmatic example not in the statement, then, but rather in the conversation conceived as the unity of meaning that grows from the interchange of question and answer.[31]

It is important to note that, like Schleiermacher, Gadamer was clear that the one who pursues understanding of another (e.g., a text) operates with preexisting expectations and preliminary judgments, or "prejudices." Any new understanding is necessarily related to one's existing horizons: "If Dasein [i.e., a located human being] is at home in its world, it is always already equipped with a knowledge of where it stands with everything, not only in relation to a future manipulation of it for purposes of providing for something but also entirely apart from that, merely to ensure that nothing unknown or unfamiliar is within the horizon of its vision."[32]

The subject's horizon is able to accommodate the "unknown or unfamiliar" only by relating it to what is already known or assumed.

Gadamer is known as the father of *philosophical hermeneutics*, and he was insistent that this enterprise is not simply about the interpretation of texts. Neither does it provide a method for the humanities, in contrast with scientific methods for the hard sciences. Rather, it is the study of that which is fundamental for all human understanding, whether scientific, artistic, critical, or mundane. It does not attempt to prescribe what we should do in interpretation, but rather, to describe what we cannot help but do in any instance of human understanding: namely, engage in specifically located dialogue.

---

[30] Gadamer, *Plato's Dialectical Ethics*, 35 (see chap. 2, n. 11).

[31] Hans-Georg Gadamer, "Grenzen der Sprache," cited in Grondin, *Introduction to Philosophical Hermeneutics*, 39.

[32] Gadamer, *Plato's Dialectical Ethics*, 22.

Ricoeur

Paul Ricoeur (1913–2005), drawing on Hegel, Dilthey, Gadamer, and others, characterized the interpreter as oneself, an "other" who enters into dialogue. This "other" is not primarily a *what* but a *who*: a "concrete person,"[33] whose life is a contextualizing narrative: "personal *identity* . . . can be articulated only in the temporal dimension of human existence."[34]

In reading word-signs, this person is neither an exalted and objective master of the text, nor purely a humiliated slave to his own conditioning, but a self-reflecting subject, who is able to perceive his own locatedness in encountering the other.

Ricoeur reflected openly on his own locatedness in encountering Christian preaching of the Bible:

> It is in terms of a certain presupposition that I stand in the position of a listener to Christian preaching. I assume that this speaking is meaningful, that it is worthy of consideration, and that examining it may accompany and guide the transfer from the text to life where it will verify itself fully.
>
> Can I account for this presupposition? Alas, I stumble already. I do not know how to sort out what is here "unravelable" situation, uncriticized custom, deliberate preference, or profound choice. I can only confess that my desire to hear more is all these things, and that it defies all these distinctions.[35]

Ricoeur was critical both of those who read texts with total naïveté (as though there were an obvious universal meaning for all readers, who are unencumbered by constraints of locatedness) and those who view the interpretation of texts with total distrust (as though the reader's power, passions, or class utterly control his or her sense of the text's meaning). Jean Grondin offered an excellent summary of Ricoeur's well-known distinction between a "hermeneutics of suspicion" and a "hermeneutics of faith":

> Along with Nietzsche as representatives of the hermeneutics of suspicion, Ricoeur names Freud, who reduces meaning to unconscious drives, and

---

[33] Paul Ricoeur, *Oneself as Another*, trans. Kathleen Blamey (Chicago: University of Chicago Press, 1992 [French ed., 1990]), 7.

[34] Ibid., 114; emphasis in original.

[35] Paul Ricoeur, "Naming God," cited in Mark I. Wallace, *The Second Naiveté: Barth, Ricoeur, and the New Yale Theology*, 2nd ed., Studies in American Biblical Hermeneutics 6 (Macon, GA: Mercer University Press, 1990, 1995), 27.

Marx, who links it to class interests. On the other side, and exhausting the spectrum, he places the hermeneutics of faith, confidence, or attestation which takes meaning phenomenologically, as it is given. Whereas the hermeneutics of suspicion looks backward, thereby reducing claims to meaning to the economy or energies that function behind them (impulses, class interests, will to power), the hermeneutics of confidence is oriented in a forward direction, toward the world that presents us with meaning to be interpreted. Such faith does not surrender to the lure of immediate meaning, however. Rather, it learns from the hermeneutics of suspicion and cooperates in destroying the illusions of false consciousness, insofar as they can be demonstrated.[36]

Thiselton

Anthony Thiselton (1937–) has been very influential in bringing the insights of Gadamer and Ricoeur (among many others) into the field of biblical studies. With Stanley Porter, I have attempted to express Thiselton's approach to hermeneutics elsewhere:

> Thiselton's contribution may be briefly—though recognizably inadequately—summarized as the attempt to illuminate the transforming engagement of the horizon of the interpreter with the horizon of the biblical text. Such a horizontal engagement must begin with the primary acknowledgment that the text to be interpreted is genuinely "other". . . . the text is an "other" subject to be encountered, rather than an object to be mastered. . . . Doing justice to the otherness of the biblical text involves attention to the entextualized "directedness" that the varied scriptural texts exhibit as products of real authors living in a real (ancient) world. . . .
>
> One of Professor Thiselton's abiding concerns is that those in modern "life-worlds" might effectively engage with the biblical texts, as the interpreter's horizon moves towards fusion with the horizon of the text. This fusion is emphatically not a bypassing of the historical gap between the Bible and the present, but rather a meeting of genuine "others," which is mediated through a tradition of "lived readings" of the text. Today's biblical interpreter is the heir of a polyphonic plurality of such lived readings, which suggest "horizons of expectation" that may be confirmed or

---

[36] Grondin, *Introduction to Philosophical Hermeneutics*, 15.

surprised in subsequent readings. The doctrines that have arisen from particular communal life-situations and have subsequently been affirmed across the history of the Church are of particular relevance, providing a provisional but coherent theological pre-understanding for those who approach the Bible. . . .

For Professor Thiselton it is essential and inevitable that the engagement of "other" life-worlds that occurs in a plurality of ongoing actualizations of biblical texts will project possibilities for surprising transformation, theological development, and future action.[37]

Jauss, Reading Contexts, and Smith

Jauss

The first encounter that a reader has with a text is always an aesthetic encounter: one finds pleasure or displeasure in reading the text. Hans Robert Jauss (1921– 1997) recognized that this aesthetic experience gives way to an acknowledgment of the otherness of the text, which then opens up the possibility of discerning the text's significance.[38]

Jauss developed an approach to interpretation known as *Rezeptionsästhetik*, sometimes translated as "aesthetic history" or "aesthetic of reception" or "reception history," related to Gadamer's emphasis on the *Wirkungsgeschichte* ("history of impacts") of a text. Andrew Talbert, whose doctoral work applied the methodology of Jauss, explains: "*Rezeptionsästhetik* functions as a summons to remain open to the content and claims of the text, to perceive the questions that the text opens for later generations, and to recognise the reader's productive role in establishing meaning."[39]

As with Gadamer, Jauss utilized the imagery of "horizons," which may be enlarged through interaction with other horizons. In the instance of a reader and a text, the reader's horizon provides the parameters of his pre-understanding, and is enlarged and transformed through engagement with the horizon of the text. His

---

[37] Stanley E. Porter and Matthew R. Malcolm, "Thiselton and Hermeneutics," in Porter and Malcolm, eds., *Horizons in Hermeneutics: A Festschrift in Honor of Anthony Thiselton* (Grand Rapids: Eerdmans, 2013), ix–xii.

[38] Hans Robert Jauss, "The Alterity and Modernity of Medieval Literature," trans. Timothy Bahti, *New Literary History* 10, no. 2 (1979): 181–229.

[39] Andrew R. Talbert, "The Reception History of 2 Thessalonians with Special Reference to John Chrysostom, Haimo of Auxerre, and John Calvin (PhD diss., University of Nottingham, 2012), 2.

very engagement with a text from the past, furthermore, is mediated through a series of other readings across history. Those readings are not to be thought of as entirely independent of the text, but *formed* by the text: they represent its impacts on those who find themselves addressed by the text.

Some trajectories of reception will prove to result in stable interpretive elements over time, while others might give way to instability and flux. An example of stability (not drawn from Jauss himself) might be the figures of Esther and Mordecai in the book of Esther: one of the features of reception of this text is its use in the annual Jewish celebration of Purim, going hand in hand with an interpretive estimation of Esther and Mordecai as heroes and models of courageous piety. Note that this estimation is not explicit within the text itself, but is a stable element of the text's reception history.

For Jauss, the later history of reception of a text need not eclipse its original meaning for its first hearers. Rather, as Talbert expressed it, "The historical . . . meaning of a text provides an aesthetic standard against which the ensuing interpretations throughout history are measured in order to determine their aesthetic value."[40]

I once heard a sermon series in which the preacher proposed that both Esther (in 'breaking the law' to enter the king's presence) and Mordecai (in refusing to bow to Haman) were acting as anti-models. Was this preacher conscious that his reading was going against the productive history of impacts of the text? If so, he did not mention it. Jauss' approach urges readers to take this post-history of the text seriously.

Reading Contexts

One of the features of hermeneutical discussion today, partly through the influence of the figures and movements we have already examined, is a heightened awareness of the productive and abusive impacts of various lived readings and appropriations of texts in their post-history. A number of feminist, womanist, liberationist, and postcolonial approaches to interpretation aim to highlight and consciously destabilize readings of biblical texts that have developed stability among readers who are perhaps ignorant of their own locatedness in strongholds of political, social, racial, ethnic, or sexual power.

Numerous reading communities attempt to foreground their own dimensions of locatedness that might otherwise be invisible in the production of biblical interpretations. This is not generally with the intention of eradicating such dimensions of located bias, but rather, of seeing them for what they are and celebrating

---

[40] Ibid., 44.

what they might contribute. An example would be the Texts@Contexts series of biblical commentaries. The series preface offers some hermeneutical reflection:

> Much of recent Bible scholarship has moved toward the recognition that considerations not only of the contexts of assumed, or implied, biblical authors but also the contexts of the interpreters are valid and legitimate in an inquiry into biblical literature. . . .
>
> Contextual readings of the Bible are an attempt to redress the previous longstanding and grave imbalance that says that there is a kind of "plain," unaligned biblical criticism that is somehow "normative," and that there is another, distinct kind of biblical criticism aligned with some social location: the writing of Latina/o scholars advocating liberation, the writing of feminist scholars emphasizing gender as a cultural factor, the writings of African scholars pointing out the text's and the readers' imperialism, the writing of Jews and Muslims, and so on. The project of recognizing and emphasizing the role of context in reading freely admits that we all come from somewhere; no one is native to the biblical text; no one reads only in the interests of the text itself.[41]

Smith

Mitzi J. Smith provides an example of foregrounding the reading context in her collection of essays on womanist hermeneutics and interpretation.[42] "Womanist hermeneutics" refers especially to hermeneutical reflection on the interpretation of African-American women. Smith noted that in recent years, womanist scholarship has been growing. She suggests that there is a need to listen to diverse voices and methodologies in biblical interpretation. She explained that in the womanist endeavor, "We audaciously start with and concern ourselves with the lives of black women and our communities."[43] This is not with the aim of pushing a new, singular, universally normative reading strategy, but to insist that this particular reading context is valid and important—both because of the real people it represents, and because of what it exposes regarding traditionally empowered reading strategies. The movement may draw attention to silenced elements of texts, marginalized voices of interpretation, and concealed agendas in traditional readings.

---

[41] Series Editors, in *1 and 2 Corinthians*, Texts@Contexts (Minneapolis: Fortress Press, 2013), x.
[42] Mitzi J. Smith, ed., *I Found God in Me: A Womanist Biblical Hermeneutics Reader* (Eugene, OR: Cascade Books, 2015).
[43] Ibid., 4.

Conclusion

A number of hermeneutical issues have emerged in this historical overview. It is worth drawing attention to one fundamental theme: that of "otherness." Hermeneutics has consistently been seen to consider the engagement of *others*.[44] This has been apparent from the dialectical approach of Plato through to the emphasis of historical criticism on the locatedness of the author and text and the current-day interest in the locatedness of the reader.

Furthermore, in the historic practice of Christian interpretation, as well as in philosophical theory in the tradition of Schleiermacher, it has been recognized that the locatedness of the reader sets parameters of *preliminary understanding*, from which they approach the textual "other" (most productively, with an orientation of inquisitive listening). Augustine, for example, consciously stood in a theological tradition that expected that the Bible would be about Jesus and would urge the love of God and love of neighbor. From this theological pre-understanding, he painstakingly listened to the text, hoping to capture the author's inner thoughts, and so find himself changed. Ricoeur, to take a very different example, consciously reflected upon his own located presuppositions and interests as he expected to be moved by an encounter with Christian preaching.

A consciousness of this complex feature of located *otherness* would seem to be the most basic commitment that the discipline of hermeneutics asks of its students.

> **BIG IDEA**
>
> The interpretation of texts involves a multifaceted encounter of others, each of which is located somewhere in time and place. The locatedness of the reader will set parameters of expectation, which may be confirmed or surprised by continued attention to the text.

---

[44] It should be acknowledged that for a number of key figures in the stream that we have focused on (philosophical hermeneutics), there is still an assumption that the "others" share some sort of correlation, which enables mutual understanding. This assumption is not shared by philosophers committed to radical transcendence, as Jens Zimmerman has pointed out: "For advocates of this radical transcendence [in the tradition of French philosopher Emmanuel Levinas], even philosophical hermeneutics, with its insistence on the historicity of our understanding, is not radically transcendent enough because it begins in correlation and strives for integration rather than difference." Zimmermann, *Recovering Theological Hermeneutics*, 7–8. In what way "others" are able to connect will be considered in the next two chapters.

Figure 1.

Questions for Discussion

1. What does it mean for the author, the text, or the reader to be "located"?

2. Is it appropriate to insist upon a "plain" reading of biblical texts? Why or why not?

3. How important is it to determine the author's intention? How would one go about doing this?

4. How relevant is the identity of the interpreter for the task of interpretation?

5. How would you make a case that there is or is not such a thing as "objective" interpretation?

6. How much weight should be given to the history of interpretation of a particular Bible passage?

7. Which historical figures from this chapter do you resonate with? Why? Are there any that you find unpersuasive?

For Further Reading

Porter, Stanley E., and Jason Robinson. 2011. *Hermeneutics: An Introduction to Interpretive Theory.* Grand Rapids: Eerdmans.

Thiselton, Anthony C. 2009. *Hermeneutics: An Introduction.* Grand Rapids: Eerdmans.

4

GENERAL AND SPECIAL HERMENEUTICS

We have seen that from the seventeenth century, hermeneutical reflection has become increasingly explicit about its universal scope, such that the nature and conditions of understanding itself have been identified as being at the heart of hermeneutics.[1] This perspective has flowered through the lineage of Schleiermacher, Dilthey, Heidegger, and especially Gadamer, resulting in what today is known as philosophical hermeneutics, which is a sort of general hermeneutics.

Thiselton has commented on Bultmann, Fuchs, and Ebeling as insisting that the Bible be understood within the purview of general hermeneutical principles: "Bultmann declares, 'The interpretation of the Biblical writings is not subject to conditions different from those applying to all other kinds of literature.' Fuchs puts the matter more theologically. How can we claim, he argues, that the biblical writings can *create* Christian faith, if we also insist that an understanding of them *presupposes* faith?"[2]

But should interpretation of the Bible be pursued from the perspective of "general hermeneutics," or does the fact that it presents itself as God's words mean that it should be treated differently? This has become a highly controversial issue in the areas of theology and biblical studies. Unfortunately, as will be seen,

---

[1] Grondin has pointed out that universality has been a de facto claim at many points across the history of hermeneutical reflection. Hence, my reference to explicit acknowledgment. See Grondin, *Introduction to Philosophical Hermeneutics*, 12–13 (see chap. 2, n. 30).

[2] Thiselton, *The Two Horizons*, 18 (see chap. 1, n. 13). Zimmermann argues that Grondin has not sufficiently acknowledged the universality of the Reformers' hermeneutics: Zimmermann, *Recovering Theological Hermeneutics*, 132 (see chap. 2, n. 24).

the discussion has sometimes involved miscommunications based on different assumptions about what general hermeneutics entails.

Hesitations about General Hermeneutics

Mark D. Thompson, of Moore Theological College, is concerned that with the general approach, "The real controls are provided by disciplines other than Christian theology."[3] Thompson cited numerous others who echo this concern, including Helmut Thielicke: "Wherever a non-Biblical principle derived from contemporary secular thought is applied to the interpretation of the Bible, the Bible's *facultas se ipsum interpretandi* [ability to interpret itself] is violated, with fatal results."[4]

Cornelis Van Dam advocates accepting a "plain" or "obvious" sense of Scripture, as an expression of faith in the God of Scripture. He argues that subordinating the Bible to a model of hermeneutics that arose from the values of the Enlightenment only serves to deprecate the status of the Bible as the Word of God.[5] Graeme Goldsworthy, an Anglican theologian, is concerned that placing the Bible exclusively within the "common arena" of a general approach to interpretation is going too far and that this is a tendency of theological liberalism.[6] He argues that Schleiermacher did not reckon with the divine inspiration of Scripture, which ought to put it in a separate category to any other text.[7] Bible scholar Hans Frei was suspicious that the generality of hermeneutics in the tradition of Heidegger, Gadamer, and Ricoeur denies the biblical text's particularity.[8]

These are some strong criticisms! Are advocates of a general approach in danger of subjecting the Word of God to human or Enlightenment or generic standards of interpretation? Where does God come into biblical interpretation?

---

[3] Mark D. Thompson, *A Clear and Present Word: The Clarity of Scripture,* New Studies in Biblical Theology 21 (Downers Grove, IL: Apollos, 2006), 118.

[4] Cited in ibid., 119.

[5] Van Dam, "Interpreting Historical Narrative," 96.

[6] Graeme Goldsworthy, *Gospel-Centred Hermeneutics: Biblical-Theological Foundations and Principles* (Nottingham: Apollos, 2006), 126.

[7] Ibid., 128.

[8] See Jens Zimmermann, "Biblical Hermeneutics," in Keane and Lawn, *The Blackwell Companion to Hermeneutics,* 212–25 (see chap. 1, n. 14).

Theological Hermeneutics?

One response to such a perceived danger is the advocacy of "theological hermeneutics," which means general hermeneutics as critiqued and enhanced by theological reflection. This is somewhat different from "theological interpretation,"
which we will consider next.

Jens Zimmerman's approach is rightly characterized as theological *hermeneutics* rather than theological *interpretation*. He echoes a theme that was seen
in our historical overview, especially in Heidegger and Gadamer (and Ricoeur,
though Zimmermann does not draw the connection): "Hermeneutics is all about
self-knowledge . . ." But to this point, which Zimmerman accepts, he adds a
theological qualification, which he draws from Calvin: ". . . and self-knowledge
is impossible without knowledge of God."[9] He reflects on the nature of the otherness that underlies hermeneutical engagement and advocates that it should be
understood in more openly theological terms than is the case in philosophical
hermeneutics.

Specifically, this otherness involves a *difference* between *persons*. The doctrine
of the incarnation shows us that transcendent *difference* has in fact been bridged;
and the doctrine of the Trinity shows us that *persons* are persons-in-relation. Our
own personhood is given to us by God, the ultimate speaking Other, and is appropriated by trust. Because of the significance of these theological foundations,
Zimmermann argues that general hermeneutics should properly be derived from
theology, rather than the other way around: there is no accounting for how "others" may truly engage, except in theology.

Zimmermann's points here seem to me to be persuasive and valuable: phil-
osophical/general hermeneutics makes use of categories that can be seen to be
theologically robust—most importantly, the nature of personhood (seen in the
Trinity) and the bridging of otherness (seen in the *incarnation*). To these two
themes I would also add the doctrine of *creation*, which undergirds the communal
and interdependent nature of humans (as seen, for example, in Gen 2:18–24 and
1 Cor 11:11–12), as well as grounding human capacity for communication in
the activity of the speaking (and accommodating) God. As philosophy professor
Craig Bartholomew has commented, "By virtue of the way God has made the
world, including human beings, being is sayable!"[10]

---

[9] Zimmermann, *Recovering Theological Hermeneutics*, 7.
[10] Craig G. Bartholomew, *Introducing Biblical Hermeneutics: A Comprehensive Framework for
Hearing God in Scripture* (Grand Rapids: Baker Academic, 2015), 29.

Theological Interpretation?

Whereas "theological hermeneutics" refers to theologically conceived *general* hermeneutics, "theological interpretation" more often refers to a *special* variety of interpretation that takes place in the context of the church and applies particularly to Scripture.

Daniel J. Treier, a Presbyterian theologian, is positive about the prospects of a theologically thoughtful approach to general hermeneutics. At the same time, he sees "theological interpretation" as describing the values that should accompany the "special hermeneutical" attention given to the Bible. The key impulses of theological interpretation for Treier include a discerning recovery of precritical exegetical instincts, an appreciation for the doctrinal "rule of faith" evidenced in early trinitarian creeds, and an affirmation of the work of the Holy Spirit in the (worldwide) church's reception of Scripture.[11]

Professor Kevin J. Vanhoozer, who focused on general hermeneutical concerns in much of his early work,[12] explicitly defines "theological interpretation of the Bible" in contrast to "a general hermeneutic." "Theological interpretation is . . . not simply a matter of imposing a *general* hermeneutic on the Bible as if the Bible could be read 'like any other book,'" he wrote. "There are properly theological questions, such as the relationship of the OT and NT, that require more than what is typically offered in a general hermeneutic."[13]

For Vanhoozer, theological interpretation is a broadly ecclesial approach to Scripture, which draws from a range of academic approaches, in studying the text as a united narrative that testifies to God's work in Jesus Christ.

Of those who advocate for some sort of "theological interpretation" of Scripture, Stephen Fowl of Loyola University is perhaps the most critical of fitting interpretation of the Bible within a general hermeneutical framework: "If one's interpretive practice is governed by a general hermeneutical theory (of any type), then it is very hard to avoid the situation where theological interpretation of Scripture becomes the activity of applying theological concerns to interpretation done on other grounds. It seems all too easy to allow a general theory of textual meaning to provide the *telos* of theological interpretation."[14]

---

[11] Daniel J. Treier, *Introducing Theological Interpretation of Scripture: Recovering a Christian Practice* (Grand Rapids: Baker Academic, 2008), 34–35.

[12] He has produced work on Ricoeur and on the contribution theology might make to epistemology.

[13] Kevin J. Vanhoozer, introduction, in Vanhoozer, ed., *Dictionary for Theological Interpretation of the Bible* (London: SPCK, 2005), 19.

[14] Stephen E. Fowl, *Theological Interpretation of Scripture* (Eugene, OR: Cascade Book), 2009), 39.

For Fowl, theological interpretation has a specifically Christian *telos*: "The ends for which Christians are called to interpret, debate, and embody Scripture are to be found in such manifestations as faithful life and worship and ever deeper communion with the triune God and with others, and that these ends neither necessitate any specific critical practice nor accord privilege to the intentions of a scriptural text's human author."[15]

Fowl reasons that these ends, rather than general hermeneutical principles, should guide theological interpretation of Scripture. They will be pursued by an open interaction of reading, doctrine, and devotional practice.

This broad movement of theological interpretation of Scripture (TIS) has come under critique. Both D. A. Carson (Reformed Evangelical theologian) and Stanley Porter (a specialist in Koine Greek grammar) suggest that the movement is unclear, disparate, and somewhat arbitrary in its convictions.

Carson[16] commends the movement's dissatisfaction with pseudo-objective, Enlightenment-bound models of historical-critical exegesis, but is concerned that theology is sometimes then pitted against history in an unsatisfying binary. He is pleased to see that theology is being brought into conversation with biblical studies, but fears that this is sometimes done uncritically and without sufficient methodological clarity. He welcomes the refreshed attention to precritical exegesis, but finds this emphasis somewhat arbitrary, overly simplistic, and not sufficiently discerning. He sees the value of acknowledging God in exegesis, but is worried that the suspicion of "human" hermeneutical rules or principles is overplayed. He applauds the instinct to read Scripture with "trinitarian lenses," but wonders whether this doctrine is an arbitrary choice. He is happy with the emphasis on the Bible as narrative, but cautions that this can be applied simplistically, with an unnecessary disdain for propositions. Carson concludes that there is not much of innovative value in this new movement.

Stanley Porter has surveyed approaches to theological interpretation by Joel Green, Daniel Treier, Stephen Fowl, and Todd Billings. He found that across these contributions, there is general dissatisfaction with historical criticism, high esteem for precritical interpretation (especially as seen in the "rule of faith"), significant regard for the church as an interpretive community, acknowledgment of the role of the Holy Spirit, and divided opinion on whether "theological interpretation" is

---

[15] Stephen E. Fowl, "Authorial Intention in the Interpretation of Scripture," in Joel B. Green and Max Turner (eds.), *Between Two Horizons: Spanning New Testament Studies & Systematic Theology* (Grand Rapids, MI: Eerdmans, 2000), 71-87; here, 73.

[16] D. A. Carson, "Theological Interpretation of Scripture: Yes, But . . ." in R. Michael Allen, ed., *Theological Commentary: Evangelical Perspectives* (London: T&T Clark, 2011), 187–207.

actually a method, and how it relates to general hermeneutics.[17] He found a lack of hermeneutical clarity and linguistic precision in a number of the works under consideration, and brings to the forefront the question of whether "theological interpretation" is in fact a coherent and sufficient hermeneutical model. His answer is ultimately negative.

While expressing sympathy with the movement's critiques of historical criticism, Porter found that in practice, proponents are divided on its continuing value for interpretation, and in fact are quite willing to co-opt other nontheological modes of analysis into their interpretive approaches. He also found that the commendation of premodern interpretation involves a simplistic grouping together of diverse approaches, which in fact included major interpretive disputes. He is troubled by the attempt to see the church as a useful control on interpretive practices, because the church is patently marked by rich diversity. He found discussions of the role of the Holy Spirit to be lip service rather than offering anything substantial.

Porter concluded that the authors he has surveyed do not promote a robust hermeneutic, although they do each (whether intentionally or not) present somewhat eclectic methods of interpretation. Elsewhere, Porter sharply distinguished the "theological interpretation" that he has critiqued from "theological hermeneutics," which he regards as the philosophically informed attempt to discern a robust hermeneutical model that coheres with the Christian theological tradition. He sees this enterprise exemplified in the work of Anthony Thiselton.[18]

A Way Forward

Rightly Conceiving of General Hermeneutics

Part of the problem is that advocates of "special" or "general" hermeneutics are sometimes speaking past each other. In practice, no one denies that there are *some* elements of complete similarity between reading the Bible and reading other texts.

---

[17] Stanley E. Porter, "What Exactly Is Theological Interpretation of Scripture, and Is It Hermeneutically Robust Enough for the Task to Which It Has Been Appointed?" in Porter and Malcolm, *Horizons in Hermeneutics*, 243 (see chap. 3, n. 37). For a response, see Kevin J. Vanhoozer and Daniel J. Treier, *Theology and the Mirror of Scripture: A Mere Evangelical Account* (Downers Grove, IL: IVP Academic, 2015), 167.

[18] Stanley E. Porter, "Biblical Hermeneutics and *Theological* Responsibility," in Stanley E. Porter and Matthew R. Malcolm, eds., *The Future of Biblical Interpretation: Responsible Plurality in Biblical Hermeneutics* (Milton Keynes, UK: Paternoster, 2013), 16–35.

The concern frequently expressed is that a "general" approach might be employed as a means of secularizing, de-absolutizing, and de-theologizing Scripture by applying universal, secular, unbelieving standards of interpretation.[19] This makes sense if "hermeneutics" is taken to mean the application of objective interpretive rules. But if the "general hermeneutical" approach is rather seen as a theologically influenced means of considering what is going on when human understanding takes place, this concern is relieved. With Stanley E. Porter, I have written elsewhere, "Hermeneutics is not a set of rules (human or otherwise) for the interpretation of texts, but an attempt to reflect at a more abstract level on how productive human understanding takes place."[20]

In this sense, interpretation of the Bible properly arises from general hermeneutics—which itself (as Zimmermann argues[21]) inherits key assumptions from its significant Christian theological prehistory—because it is conducted by humans who are pursuing understanding.

Human understanding appears inevitably to take place—as we will see further in the next chapter—by means of refining dialogue, as "others" come into contact. An effective reader of the Bible, then, whether Christian or not, will be one who approaches the Bible as an "other," ready to appreciate the distance and connections between themselves and the Bible. They will see this distance traversed by means of linguistically informed refining questioning (just as they would with any other dialogue partner).

This, I emphasize again, will be the same for those inside or outside of Christian faith or tradition. It means that, to some degree, people of various special interests and commitments can converse together about the Bible's meaning, and can even correct one another, without simply appealing to the specialized values of a particular interpretive community. For example, an atheist can inform a Christian that a specific linguistic construction has a limited scope of meaning, and that this has an impact on how a particular biblical passage should be read. A Muslim can rightly tell a Christian reader that first-century customs of head covering should impact the way a particular passage is understood. An agnostic

---

[19] See Thompson, *A Clear and Present Word*, 118.

[20] Porter and Malcolm, "Introduction to Responsible Plurality," in Porter and Malcolm, eds., *The Future of Biblical Interpretation* (Milton Keynes, UK: Paternoster, 2013), x.

[21] See above. There are others who also argue this point. John Panteleimon Manoussakis, for example, writes, "Every hermeneutics even today, be it the hermeneutics of philosophy, of art, of law, of science, and so on, has retained something of its theological origin." Manoussakis, "Hermeneutics and Theology," in Keane and Lawn, *The Blackwell Companion to Hermeneutics* (Chichester: Wiley Blackwell, 2016), 531-538; here, 531.

can correct a Christian regarding the significance of the Pauline mission for understanding the book of Philemon. Indonesian marginalized Hindu readers can
open up certain impacts of the Psalms of lament that might have been entirely
missed by a Christian community. For all readers, the normal processes of *located
attentiveness to the textual other* will occur with the Bible, bringing with them the
possibilities of comprehension and dialogue.

But, it should be acknowledged, this will not take such readers far enough,
from a Christian perspective. In chapter 1, we saw that even when Jesus's hearers
were able to follow his words, this did not guarantee that they were able to reach
the goal: "Don't you understand or comprehend? Do you have hardened hearts?"
(Mark 8:17). From a Christian perspective—indeed, from the chief character of
the Bible's perspective—what is desired is not simply "effective readers," but softhearted disciples. Further than this: softhearted disciples in community.

Rightly Conceiving of Christian Interpretation

In practice this means that Christian interpreters, while operating according to
the insights of general hermeneutics, must at some point adopt the faithful prejudice of approaching the Bible as the divinely inspired witness to their common
Lord, Jesus Christ.[22] This is the essence of Christian interpretation—that Scripture is regarded as God's Word, for God's people, about God's Son.

It is at this point that many of the values of "theological interpretation" can be
applied—although I prefer to speak simply of "Christian interpretation." Three
values in particular will be considered in chapter 7: theology, canon, and gospel.
At this point, however, it may be worth commenting on two of the movement's
other emphases: the emphasis on precritical exegetical practices and the emphasis
on the place of God/the Holy Spirit in interpretation.

In terms of the emphasis on precritical interpretation, I am in agreement with
Carson and Porter that precritical interpreters represent such a vast diversity that
it is impossible to simply affirm their approaches in general. However, the instinct
of the TIS movement that something crucial from the precritical era has been lost
in modern biblical scholarship is surely correct. Zimmermann has captured some
crucial assumptions from the premodern era: "Unlike modern Western biblical

---

[22] Later in this book, we will use the terminology of *realm* to describe this attribution of the
biblical books as divinely inspired Christian Scripture. Readers can posit different realms to which
a work of literature belongs. Christian readers will necessarily recognize that, while a work such
as Revelation may be assigned numerous valid realms (apocalyptic literature; early Christian
literature; early Jewish literature; etc.), it must at some point be regarded as God-given Christian
Scripture.

critics, Jewish and later Christian interpreters of the Hebrew scriptures assumed a world interpenetrated by the divine, and a sacred text inspired by a personal, sovereign creator God, who worked in and through history."[23]

And the late Henri de Lubac, a Jesuit priest, encapsulated the key conviction about Scripture that these interpreters held: "Jesus Christ effects the unity of the Scripture because he is its end and its fullness. Everything in Scripture is related to him. And he is its unique object. We could even say that he is the totality of exegesis."[24]

That is, premodern biblical interpreters frequently held that in the Bible the living God speaks in a unified way about his Son. This is indeed a valuable impulse for Christian interpreters to retrieve. There may be a lot to learn from the ways premodern interpreters allowed this pre-understanding to direct their readings of the Scriptures—even if we will be unable to accept all that we find. A *discerning* renaissance of interest in patristic and premodern interpretation, then, is something to be celebrated. The premoderns need not be wholeheartedly venerated simply because they are ancient; but they are frequently able to demonstrate how the essential Christian pre-understanding regarding the centrality of Christ in a unified Bible might work itself out in particular interpretive situations.

Here is an example that is special to me. In chapter 1 I cited the Venerable Bede, who suggested that hearers of the Old Testament may receive it as refreshing water (by perceiving its exemplary force), and they may furthermore receive it as gloriously transformed wine (by perceiving its typological and Christotelic value). This strikes me as an insight of astonishing depth, and it makes me want to learn more about how Bede himself put this conviction into practice. I am aware that I will need to be discerning as I look further into his work, as he is well-known for getting carried away with allegory. But I also expect that I will have much to learn from him.

This brings us to the other emphasis of TIS I mentioned: the consideration of the place of God/the Holy Spirit in interpretation. Bartholomew wrote, "Academic work, including biblical studies and theology, concentrates on analysis; Scripture asks first to be *listened to* as God's address."[25]

Bartholomew and Thomas's *Manifesto for Theological Interpretation*, therefore, emphasizes the need to receive Scripture as divine address, rather than consciously or unwittingly bracketing out the existence of God in biblical interpretation. Particular consideration is given to the role of the Spirit:

---

[23] Zimmermann, "Biblical Hermeneutics," 213.
[24] Cited in ibid. 216.
[25] Bartholomew, *Introducing Biblical Hermeneutics*, 18.

A theological understanding of God's biblical Word must be undertaken on the basis of believing in its inspired character, which means searching the Scriptures in the same Spirit in which they were written. The Holy Spirit, through whom the created human spirit obtains an understanding of God's Word, is present in the world through the church, provides the believer with the continued presence of the risen Christ, and leads all human beings through their individual and common journeys through history.[26]

But what does this mean in practice? How does one go about attending to—or failing to attend to—the voice of God or the presence of the Spirit in exegesis? Does the Christian interpreter experience these things in the construction of an academic journal article as much as in a time of corporate worship with God's people?

My own answer is that for Christian interpreters, the Holy Spirit does not enter into the process of interpretation as a separable "stage" or option. Rather, the Spirit's activity should be seen as acknowledged in the whole approach of submitting to the biblical documents as divinely given (and ecclesially received) Christian Scripture. For this reason, it makes perfect sense for the interpretive process to be marked by prayer and conducted in humble conversation with God's people; but the Bible remains God's address to humanity, whether it is studied in the academic office or in Sunday worship.

What I am advocating, then, is *general* hermeneutics (rightly—and theologically—understood), from which arises *Christian* interpretation.

BIG IDEA

If general hermeneutics refers to the study of human understanding, then interpretation of the Bible necessarily falls within its scope. Further, this field of general hermeneutics should be seen as carrying certain theologically robust concepts, such as distinct, relational personhood (seen in creation and the Trinity), and the bridging of otherness (seen in the incarnation). But while the Bible can be knowledgeably discussed by people from all manner of faiths and ideologies, Jesus himself seeks disciples who adopt the faithful prejudice of approaching the Bible as a divinely inspired witness to the Lord Jesus Christ. I call this Christian interpretation.

---

[26] Craig G. Bartholomew and Heath A. Thomas, *A Manifesto for Theological Interpretation* (Grand Rapids: Baker Academic, 2016), 21–22.

Questions for Discussion

1. In what ways is the interpretation of the Bible the same as any other sort of interpretation? In what ways is it different?

2. How should belief in God impact interpretation of the Bible?

3. How do you evaluate the theological interpretation of Scripture (TIS) movement? How do you evaluate its criticisms?

4. What can present-day interpreters learn from premodern interpreters?

5. Can the Christian church learn from non-Christian readings of the Bible? Why or why not?

For Further Reading

On Theological Hermeneutics:

Porter, Stanley E., and Matthew R. Malcolm. 2013 *Horizons in Hermeneutics: A Festschrift in Honor of Anthony C. Thiselton*. Grand Rapids: Eerdmans.

Thiselton, Anthony C. 1997. *New Horizons in Hermeneutics: The Theory and Practice of Transforming Biblical Reading*. Grand Rapids: Zondervan.

Zimmermann, Jens. 2004. *Recovering Theological Hermeneutics: An Incarnational-Trinitarian Theory of Interpretation*. Grand Rapids: Baker Academic.

On Theological Interpretation:

Adam, A. K. M, et al. 2006. *Reading Scripture with the Church: Toward a Hermeneutic for Theological Interpretation*. Grand Rapids: Baker Academic.

Bartholomew, Craig G., and Heath A. Thomas. 2016. *A Manifesto for Theological Interpretation*. Grand Rapids: Baker Academic.

5

RESPONSIBLE BIBLICAL HERMENEUTICS: GENERAL AND THEOLOGICAL FOUNDATIONS

In this chapter we will be setting out some foundations for a general hermeneutical model, in the light of key theological concepts. As seen in chapter 4, some might call this "theological hermeneutics."

The God Who Is True

It is an axiom of Christian theology that God is true. As the apostle Paul said, "Let God be true, even though everyone is a liar!" (Rom 3:4). It is, furthermore, a foundational conviction of theology that this true God is made known in Scripture.

Calvin stated, "Scripture, gathering up the otherwise confused knowledge of God in our minds, having dispersed our dullness, clearly shows us the true God."[1]

But is it possible for human language to speak with perfect truth about God? Karl Barth wrote, "If what we hear in Holy Scripture is witness, a human expression of God's revelation, then from what we have already said, what we hear in the witness itself is more than witness, what we hear in the human expression is more than a human expression. What we hear is revelation, and therefore the very Word of God. But is this really the case? How can it be? How does it come about that it is?"[2]

---

[1] John Calvin, *Institutes of the Christian Religion*, trans. Ford Lewis Battles (Philadelphia: Westminster Press, 1960), 1:70.
[2] Karl Barth, *Church Dogmatics*, I.2, ed. G. W. Bromiley and T. F. Torrance (Peabody, MA: Hendrickson, 1956 [German ed. 1938]), 473.

Even those who are suspicious of Barth's characterization of the Bible as "witness" might still have trouble imagining how finite human language can speak adequately about an infinite God: limited human language can only penetrate so far. Anglican author Michael Tinker expressed it this way: "*How* does a creator God communicate with his creation? Further, how can this be done *effectively* without the truth of what is seeking to be communicated being compromised? This problem is made more acute by the epistemological gap that appears to exist between man and God."[3]

One might initially answer that for something to be true, it need not be exhaustive or limitless. But beyond this, it is important to recognize that divine communication accommodates to human understanding.

The God Who Accommodates

The late Richard A. Norris, an Episcopal priest, found a doctrine of accommodation applied to Scripture in Augustine. "Augustine seems in the end to view the Bible on the analogy of God's self-communication in the incarnation," he wrote. "Each is a product of the humility of the eternal Word of God; for just as God's Word and Wisdom stoops for humanity's sake to take human flesh (*conf.* 7.9.13–14), so too it 'descends to the discrete bits of sound that we make' (*ad particulas sonorum nostrorum*)."[4]

Frederic Henry Chase (1853–1925) found a similar impulse in John Chrysostom, summarizing his thought as follows:

> The Bible owes its very existence to the condescension of God . . . God speaks to man in man's words . . .
>
>   As in the historical Incarnation the Eternal Word became flesh, so in the Bible the glory of God veils itself in the fleshly garment of human thought and human language.[5]

We have seen in our historical overview in chapter 2 that Thomas Aquinas had a similar perspective: God accommodates himself to human figures of speech

---

[3] Michael Tinker, "John Calvin's Concept of Divine Accommodation: A Hermeneutical Corrective," *Churchman* 118, no. 4 (2004): 325.

[4] Richard A. Norris Jr., "Augustine and the Close of the Ancient Period," in Alan J. Hauser and Duane F. Watson, eds., *A History of Biblical Interpretation*, vol. 1, *The Ancient Period* (Grand Rapids: Eerdmans, 2003), 405.

[5] Frederic Henry Chase, *Chrysostom: A Study in the History of Biblical Interpretation* (Cambridge: Deighton, Bell, 1887), 41–42.

so that humans might understand him. It is therefore fitting that divine truth is communicated in "corporeal" forms of speech.

One of the key figures to utilize in reflecting on the concept of divine accommodation in Scripture is John Calvin. In his view, God is so far above and beyond humanity that his essence is not naturally comprehensible to us. Humans are finite by nature and fallen by heredity, so we need God to stoop down to us to enable us to understand him. Calvin commented, "[God] condescends to our ignorance; and, therefore, when God prattles to us in Scripture in a rough and popular style, let us know that this is done on account of the love which he bears to us."[6]

Although the context under discussion is Jesus's conversation with Nicodemus, Calvin applied this insight to Scripture generally. Tinker commented that we "see the same logic repeatedly throughout Calvin's thought," and pointed to a number of specific examples.[7]

Note that according to Zimmermann (as we saw in the previous chapter), God's communication with humans bridges transcendent difference. Zimmermann's key image for God's effective communication with humans, then, is not *accommodation* but *incarnation*. It is worth recognizing the danger that the term *accommodation* brings—potentially miscommunicating the idea that there is such a thing as a pre-theological correlation between humans, to which God agrees to fit. Nevertheless, the image is used by major figures across historical theology, as seen earlier, and can be useful when accompanied by an awareness of Zimmermann's point: that the "human communication" to which God condescends is in fact itself theologically grounded: "the incarnate divine Logos configures reality."[8] God accommodates himself, therefore, to that which he instituted and makes possible.

The Humans to Whom God Accommodates

Just as the doctrine of the incarnation coheres with giving serious attention to what can be known about first-century history and culture, so the doctrine of accommodation coheres with giving serious attention to what can be known about human language and communication.[9] This will mean paying critical attention to

---

[6] John Calvin, *Commentary on John 1–11*, trans. William Pringle, in *Calvin's Commentaries*, repr. (Grand Rapids: Baker Book House, 1979), 17:119.

[7] Tinker, "John Calvin's Concept of Divine Accommodation," 333.

[8] Zimmermann, *Recovering Theological Hermeneutics*, 320 (see chap. 2 n. 24).

[9] Even Mark D. Thompson, who is skeptical of the value of much in modern hermeneutics, wrote that Scripture is "always and ever a piece of human communication, using all the structures and conventions of human written discourse." Thompson, *A Clear and Present Word*, 111 (see chap. 4,

the history of discussion of hermeneutics itself (as we did in chapters 2 and 3), as well as to related fields, such as linguistics and cognitive science.

Some may have reservations about opening biblical interpretation to this sort of analysis: does this dangerously deny or qualify the truthfulness or sufficiency or clarity of the Bible?

In his work devoted to scriptural interpretation, Augustine insisted that Christians should not despise the hermeneutical help that comes from "profane" disciplines: "Nay, but let every good and true Christian understand that wherever truth may be found, it belongs to his Master."[10]

Conservative theologian John Frame, a firm proponent of the inerrancy of the Bible,[11] still insists that the Bible consists of real human communication and should be studied as such: "God's speech to man is real speech. It is very much like one person speaking to another . . . God's speech is often propositional: God's conveying information to us. But it is far more than that. It includes all the features, functions, beauty, and richness of language that we see in human communication, and more."[12]

Graeme Goldsworthy, who is likewise committed to the inerrancy of Scripture, and who is skeptical of much in philosophical hermeneutics, nevertheless concedes, "If . . . non-Christians can show me something of how human language works, I regret that we cannot agree on the ultimate significance of language, but I believe I can still learn something useful from them."[13]

In this chapter, then, we will build on and extend insights from our examination of the history of hermeneutics in chapters 2–3, and the discussion of general and special hermeneutics in chapter 4. I want to draw particular attention to the significance of five related features of human communication: *otherness, openness, dialogue, refinement,* and *impact.*

---

n. 3). Thompson is concerned, however, that the application of a doctrine of accommodation needs to be tempered by the theological perspective that God himself gave language by addressing his created humans in words. Thompson is uneasy about claims or implications that human language is "inherently inadequate, open to mishearing and misinterpretation, prone to distortion and deception" (66). The perspective I am developing here is not that human language is "inherently inadequate," but that part of its very God-given adequacy is that it invites engagement.

[10] Augustine, "On Christian Doctrine," bk. 2, chap. 18, 545.

[11] "Scripture is both inerrant and infallible. It is inerrant because it is infallible. There are no errors because there *can be* no errors in the divine speech." John M. Frame, *The Doctrine of the Word of God,* Theology of Lordship series (Phillipsburg, NJ: P&R, 2010), 4:169.

[12] Ibid., 3.

[13] Goldsworthy, *Gospel-Centred Hermeneutics,* 130 (see chap. 4, n. 6).

Otherness

As seen in our historical overview, a fundamental insight of hermeneutics is that it involves "others." Hans-Georg Gadamer wrote, "Hermeneutics encourages not objectification but *listening to one another*—for example, the listening to and belonging with (Zuhören) someone who knows how to tell a story. Here we begin to glimpse the *je ne sais quoi* that we mean when we refer to people's understanding one another."[14]

It is a conviction of the church that it shares the same redemptive-historical location as the first recipients of the New Testament documents. But this does not mean that there is no distinction in horizon between today's readers and the Bible. Gadamer's point—and the point of the language of "horizons" more broadly—is not that there is a hermeneutical gap between those who are at a great historical or ideological distance from one another, but rather that *all* people and texts are located at a distance from one another. And this distance is not a problem, but an invitation to respectful dialogue.

Even those in the first-century context of the New Testament still had distance between them, which required hermeneutical sensitivity. Paul corrected a misunderstanding of his first letter to the Corinthians, saying, "I wrote to you in a letter . . . I did not mean . . . But actually . . ." (1 Cor 5:9–11). It need not be denied, then, that human communication involves differently located others and that this invites hermeneutical sensitivity.

So, *human communication involves the connection of others.*

> *2 Timothy 2:7*
>
> *Consider what I say, for the Lord will give you understanding in everything.*
>
> Notice that the fact that "the Lord will give you understanding in everything" is not a reason for Timothy to assume that everything would be instantly understandable without effort. Rather, it is a reason for Timothy to "consider" what Paul was saying, expecting that this letter would require the careful consideration that comes with engaging with an "other."

---

[14] Gadamer, foreword in Jean Grondin, *Introduction to Philosophical Hermeneutics*, trans. Joel Weinsheimer, Yale Studies in Hermeneutics (New Haven, CT: Yale University Press, 1994 [German ed. 1991]), xi; emphasis mine.

Openness

In our chapters on the history of hermeneutics, we noted that as far back as Plato, it had been considered that effective interpretation involves more than simply analyzing grammar and syntax, and so attaining an approximation of the author's intentions. That is, there are factors such as ambiguity, rhetorical cunning, and inconsistent self-awareness on the part of the speaker/author; as well as a need to recognize embodied contextual horizons on the part of the hearer/reader.

In the popular level book *Louder Than Words: The New Science of How the Mind Makes Meaning*, cognitive scientist Benjamin K. Bergen commented,

> Human language, in contrast to all other animal communication systems, is open-ended. We can talk about things that exist, like inarticulate presidential candidates and rail-thin models, or even things that don't, like Martian anthropologists or vegetarian zombies. And for the most part, other people—at least people who speak our language and have normally functioning cognitive systems—are able to understand us.[15]

Human speakers make language choices that evoke images (or simulated images) in the ideal hearer's mind, and those images color and fill out the meaning of the spoken (or written) words. This perspective reminds, of course, of the thought of Augustine (and Aristotle, though we passed over him in our historical overview).

Bergen related that polar bears have been observed to cover their noses when creeping up on seals in the snow, effectively disguising themselves until it is too late for the seals—who have poor vision—to notice them. This is intriguing: do polar bears know what they look like to seals? Whether they have adopted this out of reflective thought, or it simply arises from instinct, it is a practice that results in a successful hunt: they cover their noses, and so remain hidden from the seals' sight.

Does this scenario make sense to you? If it does, it is because your brain has supplied imagery that fills in some crucial open spaces in the story: notice that there was no reference to the whiteness of the snow, the whiteness of the polar bears' coats, or the blackness of the polar bears' noses. The scenario only makes sense to you because you automatically filled in these details according to your mind's imagery, which in turn drew on your embodied experiences (e.g., seeing

---

[15] Benjamin K. Bergen, *Louder than Words: The New Science of How the Mind Makes Meaning* (New York: Basic Books, 2012), 4.

pictures of polar bears).[16] In other words, although the scenario was not written in an abstract or poetic way, but in normal prose, it nevertheless contained elements of openness to be naturally filled in by the mental imagery of a contextually attuned reader. This is a normal feature of human communication—the human communication to which God has accommodated himself. (We are reminded here of reader-response approaches to literature, though not in their extreme form.)

Augustine, in fact, seems to have anticipated this sense of "openness" in communication—and, so, in biblical interpretation. Richard A. Norris wrote,

> Gen. 1:1 says certain things clearly, and excludes others (*conf.* 11.2.3). Nevertheless, by what it says it raises questions that a reader must and will answer, tacitly or explicitly, in order to make sense of its plain assertions and so to see what it says; and in supplying answers to these questions, different readers, as they mentally finish the text's meaning and so complement it, "see" different things. Augustine is prepared, in the *Confessions*, to apply the term "truths" to such differing interpretations (12.18.27), thus meaning not that there is no correct reading of a text, but that there is no *single* true account of its meaning.[17]

Augustine himself wrote,

> For the author perhaps saw that this very [variety of] meaning lay in the words which we are trying to interpret; and assuredly the Holy Spirit, who through him spake these words, foresaw that this interpretation would occur to the reader, nay, made provision that it should occur to him, seeing that it too is founded on truth. For what more liberal and more fruitful provision could God have made in regard to the Sacred Scriptures than that the same words might be understood in several senses, all of which are sanctioned by the concurring testimony of other passages equally divine?[18]

Augustine was not saying that everything in Scripture is open to multiple valid interpretations; simply that some parts are. This will be more obviously the case with poetic parts of Scripture. For example, that the Lord is my "shepherd" with a comforting "staff" might evoke different valid resonances with different readers (see Ps 23:1, 4). Some might be reminded that contemporary Egyptian

---

[16] This whole example is drawn from Bergen, though I have shortened it.
[17] Norris, "Augustine and the Close of the Ancient Period," 398–99.
[18] Augustine, "On Christian Doctrine," bk. 3, chap. 27, 567 (see chap. 2, n. 22).

kings presented themselves as shepherds with staffs, and so think of the shepherd-Lord as king; others might be reminded of their own experiences in correcting wayward sheep with a staff, and so think of the shepherd-Lord as corrector; still others might simply gain an overall impression of care from the image. All of these thoughts about God can be validated in other parts of Scripture, and none are ruled out by the context of the psalm.

It is worth noticing that speakers or writers are not necessarily conscious of the spaces they have left open for the hearer to fill in. Neither are they necessarily intentional about the full gamut of evocations that will spring from the impact of their words.

There may frequently be an excess or ambiguity of meaning in the speech/text, which requires and invites creative interpretation on behalf of the hearer, without being dependent on a singular intention of the speaker. This needn't mean that the text is open to an infinite number of valid interpretations; simply that it is not always tied to a singular, consciously intended meaning.

But one might interject: Is this a theologically acceptable view when we come to the Bible? Does it fit, in particular, with a Protestant view of the Bible? We have seen that figures such as Augustine were open to Bible passages having more than one meaning, and by the time of Aquinas this had developed into the expectation that each passage could communicate numerous levels of meaning (which would arise from the "literal" meaning). In the early post-Reformation period, however, Protestants became wary of the dangers inherent in a commitment to multiple meanings of each passage (particularly, the "quadriga" or fourfold interpretation), and began to speak rather of the "richness" or multipartedness of a *singular* meaning for each passage. For Old Testament passages, this richness could include typology. This is not particularly different, then, from Augustine's view: different possibilities of rich meaning arise on a passage-by-passage basis, rather than by a prior commitment to a set of multiple levels of meaning for every passage. "Openness" as I am describing it is not precluded.

It seems to me, then, that the following comment from Osborne could be aided by further qualification or explanation: "The goal of evangelical hermeneutics is quite simple—to discover the intention of the Author/author (author = inspired human author; Author = God who inspires the text)."[19]

---

[19] Osborne, *Hermeneutical Spiral*, 24 (see chap. 1, n. 9).

It is not that the intentions of the human author are irrelevant,[20] just that human communication is not exhausted by conscious intentionality. Therefore, the category of "authorial intention" needs to be carefully explained.

Augustine commented, "But which of us, amid so many truths which occur to inquirers in these words, understood as they are in different ways, shall so discover that one interpretation as to confidently say 'that Moses thought this,' and 'that in that narrative he wished this to be understood,' as confidently as he says 'that this is true,' whether he thought this thing or the other?"[21]

Will this perspective lead to the view that the author has no place and that interpretation is just the indiscriminate creation of the hearer/reader? This seems to be Goldsworthy's fear: "Postmodernism presses further with the autonomy of the individual to the point where it is the receiver who creates meaning . . . The author and the text cease to be the creators of meaning and it is left to the reader to create the meaning in the text."[22]

There may be people who take the view that Goldsworthy just described, but it is by no means a *necessary* (or common) corollary of the feature of "openness" in language and communication. It is true that, according to Gadamer, an author does not need to be fully self-aware,[23] but this is far from saying that

Here is a real-life example: I once told my Greek students, "You should generally refer to me (in Greek) as 'O Captain, my captain!'" There are a number of potential associations and suggestions in that statement, not all of which were consciously in my head when I said it:

- *Is it a joke?*
- *Does it suggest elements of the relationship between the teacher and students in the film* Dead Poets Society? *If so, what elements?*
- *Was its use a joke in* Dead Poets Society?
- *Does the title connote authority? Hierarchy?*

I honestly didn't have a single answer to these questions in my mind when I said it—and effective communication took place when the students creatively ran with it and took the excess/ambiguity of meaning where they did (using the title for formal requests, but not for general chitchat). Now, it's important that this direction is in harmony with the circumstances of the original statement, but not that its later crystallization was already in my head right at the beginning.

---

[20] Personally, I find it more precise to speak of *entextualized directedness*—which does betray the intentions of a real human author.

[21] Augustine, *Confessions*, bk. 12, chap. 24, 185.

[22] Goldsworthy, *Gospel-Centred Hermeneutics*, 40.

[23] Gadamer has pointed out: "An author does not need to know the real meaning of what he has written, and hence the interpreter can, and must, often understand more than he." Cited in Thiselton, *The Two Horizons*, 20 (see chap. 1, n. 13).

meaning is entirely open to the creative whims of the reader. I rather understand the reader to be engaging with a text in which its elements of openness participate in trajectories of textual directedness, set by a real author. The ideal reader will be unconsciously attuned to these trajectories; and the responsible hermeneut will pay critical attention to them. This would be my account of "authorial intention." Schleiermacher commented, "The elements of the language cannot be completely indeterminate, but also not completely determinate."[24]

So, *human communication between others involves "openness" that expects and invites contextual attunement.*

Mark 13:14

"When you see the abomination of desolation standing where it should not be" (let the reader understand), "then those in Judea must flee to the mountains."

Notice that Mark was conscious that the one who reads out this Gospel to the community must have the capacity to read between the lines appropriately. He very intentionally left some of his message unsaid, with the expectation that an attuned reader ought to be able to reach understanding. Jesus himself made similar conscious assumptions about his hearers at numerous points (e.g., Mark 8:17–21).

Dialogue

We saw in our overview of history that the imagery of "dialogue" between "horizons" has been especially prominent in hermeneutical discussion. Prominent thinkers such as Schleiermacher, Gadamer, Ricoeur, and Bakhtin point back to Socrates and Plato as forefathers of this perspective.

Plato was suspicious of methods of communication that avoided dialectic (i.e., dialogue). From his perspective, this meant that any written discourse was inferior to live interaction (see *Phaedrus,* 227). He did not, however, make the step to consider that the interpretation of written discourse might involve a dialectical model. This step was advocated by Schleiermacher.

It should be acknowledged that while many see the appropriateness of "dialogue" or "dialectic" as being due to the demonstrable finitude of human horizons, Schleiermacher went further and considered that this human finitude necessarily lends itself to error. Grondin commented on Schleiermacher's perspective: "This

---

[24] Schleiermacher, "General Hermeneutics," 233 (see chap. 1, n. 10).

dialectic impulse, which arises once the attempt to find ultimate foundations has been abandoned, goes hand in hand with the universalization of misunderstanding that gives Schleiermacher's hermeneutics its special thrust: the individual, intrinsically disposed to error, achieves knowledge only through conversation and sharing thoughts with others."[25]

However, I am not convinced that a necessary tendency toward *error* is the issue here; rather, it is the natural finitude of human horizons. The value of hearing several different witness reports to an accident is not simply the possibility that one or more might be in error, but more fundamentally the fact that each witness is constrained by his or her own horizons of view.

To reflect on this theologically, one might say that the Creator accommodates to finite creatures, who are by nature limited in their horizons (and who are created to share community). These finite readers encounter the Word of God with given capacities for dialogical engagement. As Zimmermann said, "To be human is to interpret. This is not a flaw but a gift; it is part of who we are."[26]

Jean Grondin encapsulated Gadamer's emphasis on a dialogical model of human understanding:

> Western philosophy's obsession with propositions involves a truncation of the most important dimension of language: its embeddedness in dialogue. To concentrate on the logical content of propositions is an abstraction from the evident fact that words have the quality of answers—that is, they are dependent on what went before, namely the question. Moreover, words have the quality of questions that invite something further, and so are dependent on what follows. In this dialectic of question and answer lies the true universality of language, from which derives the claim to universality as it is raised in hermeneutics today.[27]

This theoretical encapsulation echoes the practice of Augustine's earnest conversation with God through the Scriptures, and Chrysostom's inquisitive questioning of the biblical authors.

Of course, this "dialogue" occurs in language. We have already seen Augustine's important insight that language is *significative*. But it was flagged in our historical survey that the significative role of language has encountered some complexity in recent discussion. Recall that for Augustine, word-signs referred

---

[25] Grondin, *Introduction to Philosophical Hermeneutics*, 73–74.
[26] Zimmermann, *Recovering Theological Hermeneutics*, 165.
[27] Grondin, *Introduction to Philosophical Hermeneutics*, 37–38.

to realities, as conceived in "inner thought" or mental images. Like Augustine, Ferdinand de Saussure (1857–1913) considered not only the linguistic signifier but also the signified reality to be a mental concept, evoked by the signifier. Signs express and evoke mental images of reality, as arbitrarily assigned within language. But further, given this arbitrary cultural assignment of signification, it might be reasoned that for Saussurean thought, the cognitive *signifier* in fact precedes the *signified*,[28] such that signs are means by which humans construct reality. For example, one culture chooses to signify, and therefore "construct," certain shades of color, while another culture signifies and constructs them differently.

For Jacques Derrida, as with Saussure, signs are related to each other. But for Derrida, the observable rationality of the system is questioned. The distinction between *signifier* and *signified* is blurred, and signs refer to signs, which refer to signs, in endless signification. Thus, language resists interpretive closure.

Nevertheless, Augustine, Saussure, and Derrida are agreed that words can be used in real communication, where pragmatic understanding is actualized.

In fact, actual instances of human communication—in which people refer constantly to "this" or "that" or "there" or "here"[29]—illustrate that language use is made effective in settings of place and time. Speaker and hearer negotiate what "here" refers to with the help of extralinguistic data. The theory of signs that came from semiotician Charles Morris (1901–1979), which gives a place for the located *users* of signs, has thus led to the field of linguistic pragmatics. As Ian G. Malcolm, a professor of applied linguistics, commented, "Knowing what words and sentences mean is one thing: knowing what *people* mean is another."[30]

I therefore consider that analysis of words and their relationships *in a cultural context* is crucial to understanding. In other words, even if the weight of Derrida's problematization of interpretive closure needs to be felt, I am optimistic that the arbitrary or open elements of language do not make linguistic analysis unproductively subjective. Linguistic analysis with an awareness of cultural context does hold promise for understanding texts.

So, *human understanding progresses "dialogically," as others come into contact in language.*

---

[28] This was really the burden of French psychoanalyst Jacques Lacan, in his modification of Saussurean thought.

[29] Here I use these deictics in an "exophoric" sense—that is, making reference outside of the text.

[30] Ian G. Malcolm, "Pragmatics: The Organisation of Social Reality," in Chris Conlan, ed., *Teaching English Language in Australia: Theoretical Perspectives and Practical Issues* (Perth, AU: API Network, 2004), 139–54; here: prepublication version, 4.

> ### Acts 8:30–31
>
> *When Philip ran up to it [the chariot], he heard him*
> *[the Ethiopian eunuch] reading the prophet Isaiah, and*
> *said, "Do you understand what you're reading?"*
>
> *"How can I," he said, "unless someone guides me?" So*
> *he invited Philip to come up and sit with him.*
>
> As this conversation between Philip and the Ethiopian eunuch
> continues, the Ethiopian asks for clarification on to whom the
> prophet is referring. In this instance, then, the normally unseen
> practice of questioning a text in order to achieve understanding is
> brought into the light, with Philip presented as the authoritative
> guide.

Refinement

The question of how humans can come to know and understand something
that they did not previously know or understand is an intriguing one. Plato raised
it in a dialogue between Socrates and Meno: "[A] man cannot search either for
what he knows or for what he does not know[.] He cannot search for what he
knows—since he knows it, there is no need to search—nor for what he does not
know, for he does not know what to look for."[31]

Socrates' answer to this conundrum is that learning is really recollection
of what one already knew as an immortal soul (see both *Meno* and *Phaedo*).[32]
Schleiermacher's solution is rather that one proceeds from provisional, analogical
knowledge (that is, understanding by analogy to what is already known), to refined knowledge. Thiselton explained:

> Schleiermacher saw that what is to be understood must, in a sense, be
> already known. If this seems to involve a circularity or even a contradic-
> tion, it can only be said that this very account of understanding is true to

---

[31] Plato, *Meno*, 80e in Cooper, *Plato: Complete Works*, 880. The same issue is raised in *Theaetetus*,
which explores the relationship between knowledge and perception.

[32] Elsewhere, Plato considered the actual process of attaining knowledge in a manner very similar
to what would later be articulated by Schleiermacher: In *Statesman*, the Eleatic Stranger considers
that human (remembrance of) knowledge develops via models. He uses the example that when
children are learning to spell, they need to learn the unknown via the known. "We come to be using a *model* when a given thing, which is the same in something different and distinct, is correctly
identified there, and having been brought together with the original thing, brings about a single
true judgment about each separately and together." *Statesman* 278c; Cooper, 320.

the facts of everyday experience . . . On the one side, the child attempts
to relate a new word to what he already knows. If he cannot achieve this,
the new word remains meaningless. On the other side . . , the child has to
assimilate "something alien, universal, which always signifies a resistance
for the original vitality."[33]

This perspective reminds of Claude Bernard's famous dictum that "man can
learn nothing except by going from the known to the unknown." It also fits with
more recent insights in linguistics. Cognitive scientist and linguist George Lakoff
(1941–) argues that metaphor—using one thing to represent another thing—is
not just a matter of poetic language use, but is at the heart of human understanding: "Metaphor (that is, cross-domain mapping) is absolutely central to ordinary
natural language semantics."[34]

Metaphor is a key part of ordinary thought, and, by derivation, explains the
bulk of (English) language use. Lakoff explains: "As one gets away from concrete
physical experience and starts talking about abstractions or emotions, metaphorical understanding is the norm."[35]

For example, we speak—and think—of the body as a container: "You're full
of it"; "I've had it up to here!"; "Stop bottling it up!"; "I need some release." We
speak and think of time as a measured entity, which can be possessed: "Time is
running out!"; "I don't have time." We speak and think of writing an essay as a
journey: "I've hit a dead end"; "I've hit an obstacle"; "I've got writer's block." In
these ways we conceive of the abstract in relation to the concrete. We conceive of
the unseen (time, emotion, effort) in relation to the seen and known (containers,
possessions, travel route).

Lakoff and cowriter Professor Mark Johnson elsewhere explained that this is
because our understanding is embodied:

> We have eyes and ears, arms and legs that work in certain very definite
> ways and not in others. We have a visual system, with topographic maps
> and orientation-sensitive cells, that provides structure for our ability to
> conceptualize spatial relations. Our abilities to move in the ways we do
> and to track the motion of other things give motion a major role in
> our conceptual system. The fact that we have muscles and use them to

---

[33] Thiselton, *The Two Horizons*, 103.
[34] George Lakoff, "The Contemporary Theory of Metaphor," in Andrew Ortony, ed., *Metaphor and Thought*, 2nd ed. (Cambridge: Cambridge University Press, 1992), prepub edition, 1.
[35] Ibid., 3.

apply force in certain ways leads to the structure of our system of causal concepts. What is important is not just that we have bodies and that thought is somehow embodied. What is important is that the peculiar nature of our bodies shapes our very possibilities for conceptualization and categorization.[36]

It is instinctual—physiological, even —for humans to incorporate and understand the new via existing templates of experience. This coheres with Schleiermacher's sense that the nature of human knowledge-development is to incorporate the unknown via the known: we are "metaphorists" by nature. Thus, an "anological" or "circular" conception of human understanding need not be thought of as impossible or vicious, but as fitting with a basic feature of human cognition.

In hermeneutics, of course, this attainment of understanding, which begins with a general, provisional, analogical sense, progresses through continued engagement. A "refined" reader will therefore be at a hermeneutical advantage. Someone well versed in a text's realm (such as a fan or devotee) might be primed in productive ways of hearing the text.[37]

Years ago, I attended a mystifying piece of postmodern theater with various members of my family. At intermission, my wife, my mother, and I, a bit troubled by what we had just seen, were discussing the first act. "What on earth? What's with all the nakedness? What language were they speaking? Did anyone understand any of that?!"

Then my father, who was better versed in postmodern literature and theater, calmly piped up: "Wasn't it interesting how, in the dreamlike sequence, the man realized that he needed to leave everything he valued behind in order to make progress and enter?"

We were shocked: "What man? How did you work that out?"

As he explained, I realized that there were indeed ways of appreciating the work that I had entirely missed.

Going back a few years before that occasion, I recall my father finding a CD in my collection to which he took offense. He mentioned the title of one of the songs, and I realized that, being a nonfan, he actually had no idea how to interpret the titles, artistic motifs, and overall presentation of the band in question. On the other hand, being well versed in their material, I was able to intuitively discern elements that were tongue-in-cheek, elements that were intentionally obstructive to outsiders (cf. Mark 4:11–12), elements that were figurative, and other such guides to understanding.

---

[36] George Lakoff and Mark Johnson, *Philosophy in the Flesh: The Embodied Mind and Its Challenge to Western Thought* (New York: Basic Books, 1999), 18–19.

[37] Even Plato, who, as noted already, was suspicious of the ability of texts-without-authors to be rightly interpreted, entertained the idea that a well-versed devotee might speak on behalf of the author. In the *Lesser Hippias*, Socrates said, "Let's dismiss Homer, then, since it's impossible to ask him what he had in mind when he wrote these lines. But since you're evidently taking up

Of course, it may also be true that a fan's devotion may blind him or her to features that outsiders will notice; so it is appropriate for a fan to be self-aware of his or her own commitments and able to acknowledge other perspectives.

In applying this to the understanding of biblical texts, it needs to be recognized that twenty-first century interpreters generally stand in refined traditions of interpretation that go back many centuries, and have been systematized in creeds and theologies. As with the "fan," this holds both promise and hazards. This will be examined further in chapter 7.

So, *human dialogical understanding is oriented toward refinement.*

Mark 4:24–25

And he said to them, "Pay attention to what you hear. By the measure you use, it will be measured to you—and more will be added to you. For whoever has, more will be given to him, and whoever does not have, even what he has will be taken away from him."

Here Jesus is explicit that those who are devotees—that is, positively inclined toward him, will find in his parables further wealth about who he is and what he is doing, while those who have positioned themselves as "outsiders" will find that the parables do nothing but provide further alienation.

Impact

We saw in our historical overview of hermeneutics that Plato was highly suspicious of "sophistry," or rhetoric. Plato saw sophists as mimics of true philosophy who were experts in the art of verbal manipulation. Through the power of words, they would condemn the innocent to death and satisfy the appetites of the masses. While Plato's disdain might seem to some to be overplayed, it acknowledges the performative power of language.

The later thought of philosopher Ludwig Wittgenstein (1889–1951) provoked strong interest in the ways language use operates according to different rules in different settings. J. L. Austin (1911–1960), another philosopher, was particularly interested in "ordinary" language use. He distinguished between locutions (what is said) and illocutions (what action is performed). For example, the locution "you are husband and wife" has a particular illocutionary force when spoken by a celebrant in the setting of a wedding. Austin's work was built on by

---

the cause, and agree with what you say he meant, answer for both Homer and yourself." *Lesser Hippias*, 365d; Cooper, 925.

John Searle (1932–), who brought Austin's narrower discussion into a broader "philosophy of mind" to show that speech (or text) gives performative expression to intentionality.

In 1974, Anthony Thiselton produced an influential article, bringing the insights of speech act theory to theological hermeneutics. "Blessing and cursing are prime examples of what J. L. Austin called performative language," he wrote, "namely, a language-use in which 'the issuing of the utterance is the performing of an action.'"[38]

Thiselton did not treat speech act theory as an overall explanation of human language, but noted that its efficacy in particular usages of blessing or cursing depends on certain cultural conditions being met. Elsewhere, he was explicit that speech act theory is "one tool among many," which helps explain transformative texts.[39] The very need for such a clarification, however, shows that there has been some disagreement about whether speech act theory might provide a philosophy of language beyond Austin's narrow analysis of contextual performative utterances.

Bühler commented,

> For all concrete speech is in vital union with the rest of a person's meaningful behaviour; it is *among* actions and is *itself* an action. In a certain situation we see that a person goes at things with his hands and handles what is graspable, physical things, he manipulates them. Another time we see that he opens his mouth and speaks. In both cases the event that we can observe proves to be directed towards a goal, towards something that is to be attained.[40]

Whether or not we accept that the phenomenon of speech acts points to a general philosophy of language, it at least acknowledges and illustrates *the performative capability of human communication.*

Indeed, everyday speech shows us that communication involves action that goes beyond meanings of words, as Ian Malcolm pointed out: "When people communicate they are using a system which can bypass the linguistic form. Very incomplete

---

[38] Reproduced as Anthony Thiselton, "An Initial Application and a Caveat: 'The Supposed Power of Words in the Biblical Writings,'" in *Thiselton on Hermeneutics: Collected Works with New Essays* (Grand Rapids: Eerdmans, 2006), 62.

[39] "Speech-Act Theory as One Tool Among Many: 'Transforming Texts' (1992)" in *Thiselton on Hermeneutics*, 69–74.

[40] Bühler, *Theory of Language*, 61.

linguistic forms can convey complete messages, and linguistically complete forms can be ignored because communicators may be attending to something else."[41]

Words, sentences, and silences in communication can have an active impact. This should be taken into account in the interpretive task. If someone comments, "That's great!" it is not enough to identify grammatical forms; one must consider performative function: is this exclamation delivering the impact of an encouragement or a sarcastic put-down?

Indeed, the interpreter of the Bible may often find that technical commentaries are unsatisfying precisely because of a lack of attention to the functional or impactive dimensions of communication. One may, in fact, find that more aesthetic or "devotional" expositions are intuitively attentive to the impacts of a biblical text. Attention to these works is not necessarily, then, a sign of interpretive naïveté.

Merold Westphal, a distinguished professor of philosophy, has usefully pointed out that even limiting our attention to the entextualized intentions of the author, the active impacts of a particular saying may be pluriform: "Paul may be seen as giving words of comfort to those Galatians who have not strayed from the gospel he taught them, while directing words of warning to those who have."[42]

So, *human communication is not only informative, but performative—carrying impacts.*

Coherence

We have seen in this chapter that human communication between others involves elements of openness, inviting an engagement that can be refined through dialogue—or dialogical interpretation of a text. But communicative acts (including texts) are not *fully* open or *fully* closed, but *more* open or *more* closed. A haiku is a more open text, whereas a one-page evacuation procedure—despite being longer—is a more closed text. Both "more open" and "more closed" texts can express truth.

Furthermore, we do generally reach *pragmatic coherence* (in the sense of having sufficient confidence to believe and act) in many interpretive situations. For example, we can often sufficiently "get" what someone means, even if we don't fully understand everything that is said, and even if further examination might reveal a degree of instability in our interpretation. In terms of texts, an abstract poem tends more quickly toward meaning instability than a sign marked No

---

[41] Ian Malcolm, "Pragmatics," pre-pub 1.

[42] Merold Westphal, "The Philosophical/Theological View," in Stanley E. Porter and Beth M. Stovell, eds., *Biblical Hermeneutics: Five Views* (Downers Grove, IL: IVP, 2012), 78.

Genesis 23:10–16

Ephron was sitting among the Hethites. So in the hearing of all the Hethites who came to the gate of his city, Ephron the Hethite answered Abraham: "No, my lord. Listen to me. I give you the field, and I give you the cave that is in it. I give it to you in the sight of my people. Bury your dead."

Abraham bowed down to the people of the land and said to Ephron in the hearing of the people of the land, "Listen to me, if you please. Let me pay the price of the field. Accept it from me, and let me bury my dead there."

Ephron answered Abraham and said to him, "My lord, listen to me. Land worth four hundred shekels of silver— what is that between you and me? Bury your dead." Abraham agreed with Ephron, and Abraham weighed out to Ephron the silver that he had agreed to in the hearing of the Hethites: four hundred standard shekels of silver.

In this situation, Abraham "agreed" to pay the price for a field requested by Ephron. Except that, according to a strict analysis of his words, Ephron had not asked for a price, but rather had insisted that Abraham take the field for free! This is an example of the performative power of language in recognized contexts: everyone in the situation knows full well that Ephron has in fact stated his price in the very act of ostensibly refusing payment.

Entry.[43] Or, to use biblical examples, Job 29:17–20 inclines toward meaning instability/ambiguity far more quickly than does Matthew 27:26. This is not to comment on the *truth* of either passage, but to recognize that one passage is far more open, and one is far more closed:[44]

Job 29:17–20:

> I shattered the fangs of the unjust and snatched the prey from his teeth. So I thought, "I will die in my own nest and multiply my days as the sand. My roots will have access to water, and the dew will rest on my

---

[43] I am grateful to Alex Andrews for this example. It came in a conversation about Derrida's insistence that all texts tend towards deconstruction.

[44] One of the ways in which writers direct their readers is through their choice of genre. Indeed, an astute interpreter might *expect* that of the biblical passages cited here, the book of Job would contain more playfully resistant elements of openness than the book of Matthew, precisely because of the differences in genre.

branches all night. My whole being will be refreshed within me, and my bow will be renewed in my hand."

Matthew 27:26:

Then he released Barabbas to them and, after having Jesus flogged, handed him over to be crucified.

Varied interpreters can easily reach *pragmatic coherence* for the latter passage, in the sense that we can agree without debate that it testifies to a particular historical claim. The former passage, however, is more resistant.

Indeed, sometimes the pragmatic coherence that presumably existed between an original author and recipient(s) might be almost impenetrable for later eavesdroppers: for example, 1 Corinthians 11:10: "This is why a woman should have a symbol of authority on her head, because of the angels."

But this difficulty does not contradict the doctrine of the truthfulness of Scripture. Neither does it contradict the doctrine of the clarity of Scripture, which indicates that the Bible *as a whole* is clear enough on matters that pertain to salvation. The Westminster Confession and the 1689 London Baptist Confession echo both Augustine and Thomas Aquinas on this point: "All things in Scripture are not alike plain in themselves, nor alike clear unto all (2 Pet. 3:16); yet those things which are necessary to be known, believed, and observed for salvation, are so clearly propounded, and opened in some place of Scripture or other, that not only the learned, but the unlearned, in a due use of the ordinary means, may attain unto a sufficient understanding of them (Ps. 119:105, 130)."[45]

Our examination of language as human communication, then, is not inconsistent with viewing the Bible as infallibly true and clear for salvation. What it adds to the discussion is the nature of this medium by which God reveals

BIG IDEA

God makes himself truly known by accommodating to human language. Human language finds its ultimate source in the triune God, who created humans in his image and bridged the distance between "others" in the incarnation. This accommodation to human language means that the Bible evidences the normal features of human communication, such as otherness, openness, orientation toward dialogical refinement, and performative impact.

---

[45] Westminster Confession of Faith 1.7; 1689 London Baptist Confession 1.7. For both documents, including a depiction of their similarities and differences, see: http://www.proginosko.com/docs/wcf_sdfo_lbcf.html.

himself: it involves elements of *otherness, openness, orientation toward dialogical refinement,* and *impact.* Thus, the "ordinary means" by which Scripture is approached ought to take these into consideration, whether explicitly or implicitly.

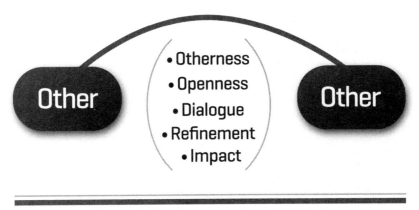

Figure 2.

Questions for Discussion

1. Read the short letter from Paul to Philemon.

   • What similarities do you see to Abraham's discussion with Ephron in Genesis 23?
   • How might Philemon have been expected to "read between the lines"?
   • How can we know, 2,000 years later, whether we are reading between the lines appropriately?

For Further Reading

Bergen, Benjamin K. 2012. *Louder Than Words: The New Science of How the Mind Makes Meaning.* New York: Basic Books.

6

A HERMENEUTICAL GOAL AND MODEL

G iven the foundations explored already (God as accommodating divine truth to human communication; and human communication as marked by *otherness, openness, dialogue, refinement,* and *impact*), we can now begin to consider a hermeneutical goal and formulate a hermeneutical model.

The Goal of a Hermeneutical Encounter

According to Gadamer, the destination of a hermeneutical encounter is the event of a "fusion of horizons," such that my own parameters are enlarged by meeting a true other. While I wouldn't use the terminology of "fusion" myself, the idea of enlarged horizons is a helpful one: "In the process of understanding, a real fusing of horizons occurs—which means that as the historical horizon is projected, it is simultaneously superseded. To bring about this fusion in a regulated way is the task of what we called historically effected consciousness."[1]

Thiselton considered how this can be a particularly positive conception for readers of biblical texts. He used the terminology of *transformation* of horizons:

> Texts . . . open new horizons for readers. Because of their capacity to bring about change, texts and especially biblical texts engage with readers in ways which can productively transform horizons, attitudes, criteria of relevance, or even communities and inter-personal situations. . . . The

---

[1] Gadamer, *Truth and Method*, 306 (see chap. 3, n. 29).

very process of reading may lead to a re-ranking of expectations, assumptions, and goals which readers initially bring to texts.[2]

Petr Pokorný, a Czech New Testament theologian, wrote, "It is a matter of the reconstruction of the reader's thinking, in which confrontation with the text and its world has led to the 'opening up' of the reader's life world."[3]

I suggest, then, that we think of the goal of a hermeneutical encounter as a *transforming engagement of horizons.* By this I mean that the interpreter will be transformed by truly engaging an "other."

In order for transformation to happen, it requires that the "other" is genuinely able to speak and is not just forced to say what I want it to say. This means that *the attentive discernment of meaning* is implied in this goal of transforming engagement.

Therefore, the best image of the hermeneut is neither the stereotypical master, who insists that his underling conform to set expectations, nor the stereotypical scientist, who dispassionately dissects and places objects under a microscope in order to explain them. If a genuine "engagement" is to occur, it necessitates a more active self-giving of the interpreter.

In an instance of effective communication or understanding, it may indeed be the case that it is not I who master the text, but the text that masters me. It may pull the rug out from under my pride, or evoke deep remorse, or excite my love, or raise my indignation, or simply expand my understanding. For Christian interpreters of Scripture, the transformation that is sought is ultimately that communities of hearers of God's Word might become more Christlike.[4]

I find it useful, then, to adopt a model of hermeneutics that sees the interpreter as an inquisitive interviewer, engaged in a communicative act.

A Model of Hermeneutics

Drawing on the foundations developed in the previous chapter and the historical discussion of the chapters before that, I propose the following model of hermeneutics—which is really just a combination of the image of "other horizons" with the image of the hermeneutical circle. Note that this is not a method for exegesis,

---

[2] Thiselton, *New Horizons*, 8.

[3] Petr Pokorný, *Hermeneutics as a Theory of Understanding*, trans. Anna Bryson-Gustová (Grand Rapids: Eerdmans, 2011), 184.

[4] Here I am entirely in agreement with the goal of theological interpretation outlined in Bartholomew and Thomas, *A Manifesto for Theological Interpretation* (see chap. 4, n. 26).

but a model of effective human understanding, particularly applied to biblical texts.

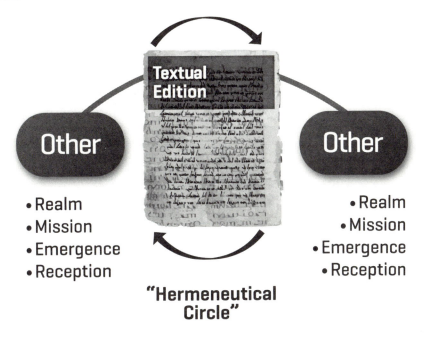

Figure 3.

The hermeneutical task involves seeking a transforming engagement between the text and the reader. It involves a refining questioning of the text (from the level of the word to the level of the discourse[5]) in a way that is primed with an appreciation for its realm, mission, emergence, and reception, as well as an acknowledgment of the reader's own realm, reading mission, emergence, and traditions of reception. Each of these dimensions represents a facet of the locatedness of text or reader. Note that in this diagram the refining questioning of the hermeneutical circle occurs with a particular *edition* of the text (whether in Hebrew, Greek, English, or another language), which is recognized to have arisen from the text's post-history.

---

[5] Note that Stanley Porter also proposes attention to "clausal semantics and discourse semantics" as an essential element of the hermeneutical task. Porter, "Biblical Hermeneutics and *Theological Responsibility*," 23 (see chap. 4, n. 18).

We will now spend some time exploring the facets of locatedness utilized in this model.[6]

Realm

This is really the broadest articulation of categories of pre-understanding. A particular interpreter, given his or her own locatedness, might provisionally consider the realm of a particular text to be the songs of AC/DC; or, a textbook; or, the *Washington Post*; or, early Christian literature; or, the New Testament. It is inevitable that the interpreter will bring some sort of provisional answer to the question of realm in order to approach a text. This realm may be complex and is bigger than "genre." Remember: Schleiermacher noted that attention to the general is both essential and inevitable. As Jauss pointed out, the reader's initial sense of a text will generally be aesthetic rather than analytical.

At the same time, the interpreter belongs to his or her own realm. Although the question of one's identity is unquestionably broad and complex, it is unavoidable that the interpreter be regarded as, in general ways, "other" to the text. For example, if I am to read a book, at some level I need to recognize that I am not in fact the book myself! I am Matthew Malcolm, with all that that identity entails.

Mission

The *mission* of the text is its broad performative orientation. One might ask, "To what broader mission does a Lee Strobel book about Jesus contribute?" or "What might be the broad

If we have an unclear initial sense of what a text is, we lack reference points with which to interpret it. As I was packing up boxes of our books to take from Australia to Indonesia, I came across one called A Student's Handbook of Housewifery. *I had no recollection of seeing this book before, and no idea how it got among our books. Given that I had pulled it out from between a couple of comedy books, I had a suspicion that it might be a satire. I opened the front cover and read: "This book is bound in washable cloth. Sponge lightly to clean." This confirmed my suspicions: the book must be a humorous take on an early-twentieth-century-style "woman's guidebook." But then I noticed that the date on the book was 1940, and it did appear quite old. Was this part of the joke, or was it real? As I flipped through the book, I couldn't quite work out whether the overly thorough instructions on cleaning were supposed to be taken seriously or not. I had no idea how to interpret the book! I have since come to the view that it is a real, serious guidebook. But I still have no idea how it came into our possession!*

---

[6] There is some overlap between the material in this section and my chapter in *The Future of Biblical Interpretation*, where I also addressed *realm, mission, emergence,* and *reception* (see chap. 4, n. 18).

project of Bart Ehrman's work?" or "How might we characterize the larger enterprise of which Martin Luther was a part?" The more familiar we become with a text and its contexts, the better attuned this sense will become. This is bigger than the "occasion" of a text, and it might be unconscious for the author. (For example: would Strobel, Ehrman, and Luther agree with your assessment of their broad projects?) Perceiving the mission of a text will involve careful attention to subtle elements within the text, as well as factors outside of the text. The interpreter who is especially attuned to this dimension will be well equipped to read between the lines of the text or think imaginatively about where the trajectory of a work's ideas might lead.

At the same time, the interpreter participates in some sort of "reading mission" in interpreting the text. There is, of course, no such thing as an objectively neutral reader. This is especially true with regard to biblical texts, though it is not always the case that the reader is self-critically conscious of what outcomes he or she hopes will arise from each encounter with the text. For example, one reader might look up some song lyrics as a fan, with the intention of being better able to sing along. Another reader might look up some song lyrics as a suspicious parent, expecting to find questionable material. These respective reading missions will impact the way the lyrics are read. The same could be said with regard to readers of the Bible.

Emergence

The reader considers the *emergence* of the text in space, time, and language. Whether consciously or not, it is unavoidable that the reader encounters the text as arising in a particular language, from a particular location. This wide-ranging issue has dominated the last two centuries of biblical interpretation, and in the early 1800s, Schleiermacher rightly noted that for the self-aware interpreter, questions of genre, authorship, occasion, and language are important:

I live in Indonesia, but I am only beginning to learn the Indonesian language. I am therefore sometimes painfully aware of the linguistic and cultural assumptions that I am liable to bring to any piece of Indonesian speech or writing that I need to decipher. I am much less self-aware when reading English language texts.

"Everything in a given utterance which requires a more precise determination may only be determined from the language area which is common to the author and his original audience."[7]

---

[7] Schleiermacher, "Hermeneutics and Criticism," 30 (see chap. 1, n. 10).

At the same time, the related elements of the interpreter's own locatedness can be given articulation, particularly in terms of language and culture. It may happen on occasion that these elements of the reader's locatedness are foregrounded in an act of interpretation, where areas of connection or disconnection present themselves, or where there is discussion with other-located readers.

Reception

The interpreter encounters the text at some point in its post-history. With relation to the Bible, generations of interpreters have already developed reading traditions, passing on their discoveries and difficulties to subsequent generations. Some of these traditions have become stable over time, while others may now appear quaint and time-bound. The present-day interpreter will find his own assumptions and questions shaped, altered, and resisted by such traditions. The first point of contact between the present-day interpreter and an ancient text is never the text itself, in an untouched state, but rather, the text as mediated by intervening generations. For the Bible, this mediation includes the addition of chapter and verse divisions, as well as stabilized assumptions about meaning. The responsible and self-aware interpreter will want to perceive where such concretized readings have been fruitful, suggestive, or abusive.

At the same time, the interpreter has some cognizance of the traditions of reception in which he himself stands, or which he resists: perhaps he holds to the Christian creeds as a "rule of faith." Perhaps he belongs to a confessional tradition or institution. Perhaps he is consciously hurt by reading traditions from a particular perspective. Perhaps he is self-consciously secular in his approach.

Questioning

In the context of the previous features of the contextual locatedness of both the text and the reader, the interpreter approaches the text with questions (conscious or otherwise) about language choices in the text, from the level of the word to the level of the whole discourse: "What does that mean?" "To whom are you referring?" "Why phrase yourself that way?" "Is that an insult?" "How does this relate to what you said earlier?" When rigorously articulated and applied to Scripture, this normal linguistic exercise is the basis of what we call *exegesis* (see the definition in chapter 8).

This is conducted with a view to a transforming engagement of horizons. Launching from the pre-understanding shaped by the various features of locatedness explored previously, the interested questioning refines the reader's initial understanding, which in turn refines the questioning, as the reader stands ready to be moved by the textual encounter.

Application of the Model

Hermeneutical Self-Awareness

Much of this happens instinctively, with varying degrees of self-awareness and responsibility. The history of hermeneutical discussion would suggest that where facets of locatedness are downplayed or ignored, fruitful interpretation may be in jeopardy. For example, an interpretation that ignores the productive history of reception of a text may prove idiosyncratic and unpersuasive. That is not to say that a text's reception cannot be *defied*; but for responsible interpreters it will at least be *engaged*. Similarly, an interpretation that ignores the culture in which the text arose may prove misguided. An interpretation that fails to recognize the interpreter's own cultural locatedness may prove narrow or naive.

The value of this model, then, is simply that it brings into (partially) conscious analysis those features of locatedness and communication that might otherwise be missed or assumed. It is not, in itself, a method of exegesis, but rather attempts to picture simply key factors at stake in interpretation. The model might be applied by allowing it to guide hermeneutical self-awareness when approaching an instance of interpretation of the Bible (or another book, or a movie, or a song, or a play . . .). It ought to bring clarity to questions of what the text meant in its initial contexts and how it might exert its impact today.

Application to a Study of "the Bible and Sexuality"

Here is how I attempted to apply this model when I was asked to address the issue of "Paul and sexuality" for a denominational conference. In preparing to address the issue. I did three things.

1. I tried to be consciously attentive to the Pauline horizon.

Realm: I recognized that I was approaching the Pauline literature *both* as first-century ethical literature (and so profitably considered in terms of first-century conventions, and compared with other ancient literature from the time) *and* as Christian Scripture (and so uniquely true, canonically contextualized, and essentially related to the gospel of Jesus Christ).

Mission: I articulated my sense of the Pauline mission out of which Paul's documents arose: this apostolic mission was one in which Paul sought to bring

Jews and Gentiles from Gentile territory into maturing submission to Jesus Christ as risen Lord, in community with one another. I was conscious that the specific passages being analyzed should not be divorced from this context.

Emergence: I considered other ethical discussions of Paul's time, such as Seneca's discussion of "passions," and other ancient accounts of sexuality. I studied these, as well as the Pauline material, in critical editions. I spent a great deal of time studying artifacts and secondary discussion of the relevant ancient cultures. For example, what were first-century Greco-Roman views on topics such as pederasty? How did they understand marriage? Did they have same-sex relationships? If so, what did they call them? What Greek or Latin words were relevant in their own contexts?

Reception: I looked into the history of discussion and impacts of the key passages. I attempted to consider trajectories of reception that were in sympathy with the biblical texts, as well as those that were hostile to the texts.

2. I tried to be attentive to my horizon.

Realm: I articulated my own self-identification as Christian, and also recognized that I do not self-identify as homosexual. I wrestled with whether "straight" is a useful self-identifying term. I ended up including an honest discussion of my own self-identification in the paper that I presented.

Mission: I acknowledged the weight invested in this issue by those who had invited me and another speaker to address their denomination. I consciously grappled with the expectation that I would provide a "conservative" voice (which is what I believed the organizers expected). To some extent, this resulted in my consciously trying out views that were resistant to the organizers' expectations of me—because I didn't want to simply engage in an interpretive exercise that was "rigged" in a particular direction. But as I worked on the texts, I did find myself coming to traditional conclusions about the passages in question, and I was open about these dimensions of my reading mission with my audience.

Emergence: I recognized that my society (in twenty-first-century Western Australia, where I lived at the time) was one that valued diversity and tolerance, and one with a vocal and interested alternative-sexuality community. I therefore met with a number of representatives of Perth's queer community to hear their perspectives. I also read a number of books on related topics by self-identifying queer authors. I acknowledged (to myself more than to others) the pressure I personally felt to deliver exegetical findings that would not be laughably regarded as outdated or bigoted. I tried to be aware of whether this pressure was causing me to adjust my outcomes.

Reception: I considered the weight and value of the theological tradition from which I come, and spoke with others within this tradition about the issue. I sought their advice and was optimistic that there would be voices within this tradition carrying worthwhile perspectives. I also sent my intended paper to people from entirely different traditions and opposing perspectives, inviting their feedback. My aim was that I would value my own tradition, but also have it stretched and challenged by alternative perspectives.

3. I tried to be attentive to the texts.

In the context of this attention to facets of my horizon and of the texts' horizon, I examined and questioned numerous biblical texts, which included passages from Romans and 1 Corinthians. I attempted to understand the morphology, syntax, semantics, and pragmatics of the language used.[8] In other words, I conducted exegesis. I made use of the Nestle-Aland Greek New Testament, Rahlfs's *Septuaginta*, and several English translations.

After doing my own work on the passages, I also consulted commentaries to hear from others who had worked on the same passages.

I tried to bring all of this attentiveness to bear on the question facing the denomination: how should they hear Scripture speaking to their situation today? All of the contextual and interpretive resources aimed toward this matter of a *transforming engagement of horizons*. My hope was that I was doing exegesis with my eyes open to the hermeneutical issues at play in the exegetical endeavor.

> **BIG IDEA**
>
> A successful hermeneutical encounter is something like an interview, in which the interpreter reaches refined understanding by asking questions of the other (in our case, a text). Whether consciously or not, this involves some acknowledgment of the locatedness of both interpreter and text. This locatedness might be examined and fleshed out, using the categories of realm, mission, emergence, and reception.

Questions for Discussion

1. How might the interpretive task be different if it is envisaged as being like

    -   a master directing a servant?
    -   a scientist dissecting an insect?
    -   a reporter interviewing a person?

---

8 These categories will be further unpacked in chapter 8.

2. Consider the Bible as a key text:

   • What different "realms" might validly be posited for different parts of the Bible?

   • How would you describe the "missions" behind different parts of the Old and New Testaments?

   • How much do you know of the "emergence" of the biblical texts? How important do you think this is? Is it important to know the biblical languages?

   • How would you find out about the "reception" of a particular Bible passage over the past 2,000 or so years?

3. Consider your own situation:

   • How would you describe your own "realm"—that is, how would you answer the general question, "Who are you?" How might this affect your reading of the Bible?

   • How would you describe your own "mission" in reading the Bible? Do you think you generally approach the Bible to hear God's voice? To obey it? To discredit traditional Christianity? To defend traditional Christianity? You might have several answers. How might this affect your reading of the Bible?

   • How would you describe your own "emergence" in time and place? What languages do you speak? With what cultures do you associate? Where are you located? How would you identify yourself in terms of ethnicity and sexuality? How might these things affect your reading of the Bible?

   • How would you describe your own traditions of reception? Are there particular traditions of Bible use with which you strongly identify? How might this affect your reading of the Bible?

For Further Reading

Brown, Jeannine K. 2007. *Scripture as Communication: Introducing Biblical Hermeneutics.* Grand Rapids: Baker Academic.

7

FRUITFUL INSTINCTS FOR THE INTERPRETER
OF CHRISTIAN LITERATURE

The model of hermeneutics that we examined in the previous chapter does not necessitate a singular method for interpretation of biblical texts. The model does urge an orientation of self-aware, active inquisitiveness, and we will examine useful interpretive impacts of such an orientation in the next chapter, when we move "from hermeneutics to exegesis." But it would seem useful, first, to consider how the general hermeneutical model might be combined with fruitful instincts for the interpreter of Christian literature. In particular, we will be interested in those who practice interpretation of Christian literature from the inside.

It was said in chapter 4 that "Christian interpretation" arises from "general hermeneutics," resulting in an approach to the Bible that might be described as the faithful prejudice of holding it to be God's united witness to the church's common Lord, Jesus Christ. In this chapter, we will unpack three facets of such pre-understanding: *theology, canon,* and *gospel.*

Theology

The provisional system that systematic theology provides for the interpreter honors a centuries-long heritage of biblical interpretation by setting faithful prejudices in approaching the text. Such prejudices are, in turn, open to refinement by careful exegesis.

We have seen already that this was openly the case for patristic, medieval, and Reformation interpreters. It may also be seen in the way the New Testament writers read their Old Testaments (as will be further explored in chapter 10). Anthony

Thiselton pondered the issue: "If the New Testament writers approached the Old Testament in the light of a pre-understanding that was theologically informed (for example, by Christology), does this not mean that in order to be true to the tradition of the New Testament itself the interpreter will consciously approach the text from a particular theological angle?"[1]

Moisés Silva, who has served as translator for a number of Bible translations, commented on the example of John Calvin in this regard, insisting that the reader of his commentaries should be familiar with his *Institutes*: "My own thesis is that both his expositions and his theology are superb precisely because they are related," he wrote.[2]

For much of history, then, practitioners of scriptural interpretation have self-consciously had their reading of Scripture guided by a systematic theological pre-understanding. In terms of a theoretical understanding of the relationship between doctrinal coherence and exegetical openness, however, recent developments are rather interesting.

Mikhail Bakhtin (1895–1975), the twentieth-century Russian philosopher and literary critic, explored the interplay between particularity and coherence in human language and novels. Finding notable heritage in Socratic dialogue,[3] he commended the concept of *polyphonic* concordance: there may be various "voices" in human language or a novel, each speaking distinctively, and yet contributing somehow to a complex whole. He described the complexity of the novel as follows:

> I find three basic characteristics that fundamentally distinguish the novel in principle from other genres: (1) its stylistic three-dimensionality, which is linked with the multi-languaged consciousness realized in the novel; (2) the radical change it effects in the temporal coordinates of the literary image; (3) the new zone opened by the novel for structuring literary images, namely, the zone of maximal contact with the present (with contemporary reality) in all its openendedness.[4]

---

[1] Thiselton, *The Two Horizons*, 23 (see chap. 1, n. 13).

[2] Walter C. Kaiser Jr. and Moisés Silva, *Introduction to Biblical Hermeneutics*, rev. and exp. ed. (Grand Rapids, MI: Zondervan, 1994, 2007), 303.

[3] M. M. Bakhtin, "Epic and Novel," in *The Dialogic Imagination: Four Essays*, ed. Michael Holquist; trans. Caryle Emerson and Michael Holquist (Austin: University of Texas Press, 1981), 24–25.

[4] Ibid., 11.

In the twenty-first century, one might also point to the lifelike plurality of interacting voices in television drama, with which viewers find deep and complex connection. Is it possible to summarize what Downton Abbey was about, without being entirely bland and general? And yet, in its complexity, it did have definable borders and key themes.

Bakhtin himself did not apply his polyphonic understanding of the novel to the Bible. In fact, as an authoritative canon, the Bible might seem to be strongly resistant to some of the freedom and openness[5] with which Bakhtin characterized the novel. Nevertheless, a number of scholars have seen potential in his polyphonic approach for a consideration of the nature of biblical coherence. Anthony Thiselton commented,

> Mikhail Bakhtin (1895–1975) draws on philosophy, literary theory, theories of communicative action, aesthetics, and even post-Einsteinian physics, to formulate an understanding of communicative action through multiple voices that is more than fruitful for discerning how diversity within the canon nevertheless leaves ample room for legitimate theological construction, albeit of an 'open' and ongoing kind.[6]

We see here a theoretical account that coheres to a certain extent with the historic instinct of Christian interpreters to utilize their systematic theology in pursuing the study of the Bible. That is, a sense of canonical coherence is provisionally entertained by the interpreter at the same time as an attendance to the particularity of each scriptural passage's unique "voice."

To simplify: it need not be a conviction of Christian interpreters that every text has to sing in unison about the gospel to be a part of the scriptural choir. Disparate elements and apparent loose ends may still be part of an overall polyphonic coherence.

Thiselton likewise said that the Scriptures "often speak with plural or 'polyphonic' voices. To expect otherwise is to forget that at the very heart of hermeneutics stands a dialectical relation between particularity and universality between

---

[5] When other genres are influenced by the novel, Bakhtin stated that they "become more free and flexible, their language renews itself by incorporating extraliterary heteroglossia and the 'novelistic' layers of literary language, they become dialogized, permeated with laughter, irony, humor, elements of self-parody and finally—this is the most important thing—the novel inserts into these other genres an indeterminacy, a certain semantic openendedness." Ibid., 7.

[6] Anthony Thiselton, in Craig Bartholomew et al., eds., *Canon and Biblical Interpretation*, Scripture and Hermeneutics series (Milton Keynes, UK: Paternoster, 2006), 7:25.

contingency and coherence, and between a plurality of interpretations and a stable core of tradition."[7]

Systematic theology provides an attempt to discern the chief melodic motifs of the scriptural symphony. Even if Bakhtin's model of the novel cannot be applied to the Bible *in toto*, it opens space to consider how it is appropriate for Christian interpreters to hold to their inheritance of systematic theology when they engage in biblical interpretation: they are holding to a provisional, guiding conception of the whole, while allowing space for genuine polyphony. In turn, the polyphonic voices of Scripture refine the systematic conception.

I am almost in agreement, then, with the axiom cited by Van Dam: "Scripture must be interpreted through the spectacles of Scripture; the pre-understanding with which the interpreter approaches Scripture must wholly conform to Scripture. This hermeneutic circle must be consciously embraced."[8]

My hesitation with this formulation is that "pre-understanding," by definition, is *my* preliminary sense. It is certainly appropriate to say that the pre-understanding with which the interpreter approaches Scripture should be submitted to, and refined by, Scripture. But to phrase it as Van Dam did comes close to concealing one's own locatedness, and thus denying the hermeneutical circle as it really is. It is not *Scripture's* pure pre-understanding, but *Matthew Malcolm's* scripturally refined pre-understanding that I bring to the Scriptures. And Matthew Malcolm finds himself standing in, and influenced by, particular theological traditions, in his systematic grasp of Scripture's message.

Canon

This brings us to a consideration of canon. The canon defines the boundaries of the voices to be considered as contributing to the polyphony of Christian Scripture. This does not, of course, mean that the interpreter of Christian Scripture will only pay attention to canonical documents; but it demarcates a key "realm" that Christian interpreters will hold in their pre-understanding of any specific scriptural text.

With long historical precedent, Christian pre-understanding considers Genesis or Psalms or Isaiah or Matthew or Romans or Revelation to belong to the "realm" of the Christian canon. (It may concurrently belong to other realms, but

---

[7] Anthony C. Thiselton, "Resituating Hermeneutics in the Twenty-First Century" in *Thiselton on Hermeneutics: Collected Works with New Essays* (Grand Rapids: Eerdmans, 2006), 40.

[8] Van Dam, "Interpreting Historical Narrative," 101 (see chap. 3, n. 11).

for Christian interpretation, the Christian canon is necessary at some point.[9])
This perspective is implicit in the assertions of Augustine, Thomas Aquinas,[10] the
Westminster Confession, and the London Baptist Confession that Scripture *as a
whole* is able to speak clearly, because those parts that are unclear are balanced by
other parts that speak of the same doctrines more plainly.

This means that the "insider" or "fan" who interprets Christian literature will
be highly attentive for resonances and interactions between canonical voices, but
need not rush to bring unison between every element. In these varied resonances
and interactions, the Christian interpreter will find polyphonic direction. Two
major themes are worth considering as examples: *kingdom* and *covenant*.

The theme of kingdom begins in the first chapter of the Bible, in which the
divine ruler appoints humans to have creative dominion over his realm. They
turn from God and thus find their position frustrated, but the divine ruler is
not finished. He acts as King of a chosen people, Israel, leading them through
the desert to a land of their own. There, he aligns his own kingship to that of the
shepherd David, and promises that David's son will be his own son. High hopes
for Solomon are dashed when he turns to idols, but the prophets' condemnation
of subsequent kings' idolatries are outshone by their promises that the kingdom
of God will one day be established. Jesus arrives on the scene at the outset of the
New Testament, announcing that the kingdom of God has arrived—but with un-
expected timing (beginning in apparent ignominy, and destined for an astonishing future harvest); and a surprising son of David (who must suffer, die, and rise
on the third day). One day, the kingdom of this world will become the kingdom
of our God and of this Messiah.

The theme of covenant likewise begins at the beginning of the Bible, as God
is shown to speak promises that define relationships. At a crucial turning point,
he makes a covenant with Abram, promising that through Abram's descendants,
the whole world will be blessed. His descendants go on to receive further promises in the Sinai covenant: Israel will be the Lord's own special people, and he will
be their God. While the prophets bitterly complain that the people continually
break their covenant obligations by their unfaithfulness, they remind the people
that God has also made a covenant with David regarding his son; and they look

---

[9] Which Christian canon, of course, will be defined by the respective Christian traditions.

[10] Indeed, Dr. Christopher T. Baglow of Notre Dame Seminary, noted that canonicity is "funda-
mental to his approach, and has important ramifications for his actual practice." Baglow, "Sacred
Scripture and Sacred Doctrine in Saint Thomas Aquinas," in Thomas G. Weinandy, Daniel
Keating, and John Yocum, eds., *Aquinas on Doctrine: A Critical Introduction* (London and New
York: T&T Clark, 2004), 6.

ahead to the time when God will establish a new covenant. Jesus points to his own death as the inauguration of the promised new covenant. The New Testament looks ahead to the time when this covenant will fully flower in a new creation of all things, as the people Jesus has gathered "will be his peoples, and God himself will be with them and will be their God" (Rev 21:3).

These two crucial themes, which stretch across Old and New Testaments, exemplify the rich intertextuality, narrative development, and subtle typology that the canon-conscious Christian interpreter may find in the Bible.

Further than acknowledging that canon provides parameters for such intertextuality and development, the Christian interpreter can also ponder order and meaning within the structures of the canon. For example, one might consider the significance of the Christian Old Testament canon ending with Malachi. One might consider the effects of the canonical arrangement of the Psalms or the meaning of having four canonical Gospels. The Christian interpreter will not just acknowledge that these features exist, but will ponder why God has chosen to speak to his people in these ways, and what they might communicate.

Gospel

Gospel as Center

The father of modern canonical interpretation, Brevard Childs, stated that the historic Christian view is that the canon is "grounded in a christological center revealed in a historic incarnation."[11] Indeed, my account of the themes of covenant and kingdom in the previous section betrays my theological conviction that while *canon* demarcates the boundaries of the polyphonic voices of Scripture, the *gospel* of Jesus Christ describes their provisional center, giving us a way of reading the canon *Christianly*.

The very possibility of having a fixed "center" sits in tension with Bakhtin's understanding of the "openendedness" of the novel, but need not be thought of as an impossibility within a polyphonic canon, particularly if that center is conceived as key plurally witnessed news about a dynamic person (i.e., Christ) rather than a one-dimensional theme.

Irenaeus discerned, from the four Gospels, key elements of *the* gospel, which must guide those who would interpret "the Gospels of the Apostles": that the one

---

[11] Brevard S. Childs, "The Canon in Recent Biblical Studies," in Bartholomew et al., *Canon and Biblical Interpretation*, 41.

God is Creator, speaker, lawgiver, and Father of Jesus Christ. "Such, then, are the first principles of the Gospel: that there is one God, the Maker of this universe; He who was also announced by the prophets, and who by Moses set forth the dispensation of the law,—[principles] which proclaim the Father of our Lord Jesus Christ, and ignore any other God or Father except Him."[12]

He later added that this testimony is confirmed by the other apostolic writings: "that He was the Maker of all things, that He was the Father of our Lord Jesus Christ, that He was the God of glory."[13]

In other words, despite having notable particularity, the accounts of the Old and New Testaments have a unity in the one God, who creates, speaks, rules, and is Father of Jesus Christ.

We have already seen that Augustine held that the Bible testifies to Christ, and that those who interpret it in a way that contradicts love for God or neighbor are misinterpreting it. We have seen that Bede understood the Old Testament to be like refreshing water in its moral witness for believers, and like wine when its Christotelic function is recognized. We have seen that Luther insisted that the whole Bible must be understood in terms of its witness to Jesus Christ, by means of "law" (as a foil for grace) and "gospel" (as the expression of grace). We have seen that Calvin understood the Bible to bear witness to Jesus Christ through a salvation-historical narrative in which full disclosure of the gospel was deferred until the time of Jesus Christ. The great Baptist preacher Charles Spurgeon called for his students to take note of how each part of Scripture related to the gospel:

> It will be a happy circumstance if you are so guided by the Holy Spirit as to *give a clear testimony to all the doctrines which constitute or lie around the gospel*. No truth is to be kept back . . . Harmony requires that the voice of one doctrine shall not drown the rest, and it also demands that the gentler notes shall not be omitted because of the greater volume of other sounds. Every note appointed by the great minstrel must be sounded, each note having its own proportionate power and emphasis.[14]

By any estimation, these views include key figures in Christian history, variously voicing the instinct that the Bible needs to be approached with the

---

[12] Irenaeus, *Against Heresies*, bk. 3, chap. 11, pt. 7; in Alexander Roberts and James Donaldson, eds., *Ante-Nicene Fathers* (Peabody, MA: Hendrickson, 2004 [original 1885]), 1:428.

[13] Irenaeus, *Against Heresies*, 3.12.11, in ibid., 434.

[14] C. H. Spurgeon, *Lectures to My Students: Complete and Unabridged* (Grand Rapids: Zondervan, 1954), 74–75; emphasis in original.

theological assumption that it is the one God's united witness to Jesus Christ. The weight of the Bible's impact on Christian readers demands consideration. But are these figures hearing a united emphasis that derives from the biblical documents themselves, or are they bringing an artificial theological unity to those documents? We need to consider whether the biblical documents themselves suggest a gospel-centered unity.

Gospel in the New Testament

While the attempts by form critics in the early twentieth century to discern a primitive apostolic *kerygma*[15] were at times marked by the downplaying of polyphony or a determination to find set forms,[16] the New Testament itself does give some reason for considering "gospel" as a key to the Christian Scriptures.[17]

In 1 Cor 15:1–5, Paul indicated that the "gospel" he had received and passed on was "most important," encapsulating the essential news that Christ died for sins according to Scripture, was buried, was raised on the third day according to Scripture, and appeared to Cephas and the Twelve. Paul referred by name to other "apostles" (v. 7) and insisted that "whether, then, it is I or they, so we proclaim" (v. 11).

In 1 Pet 1:10–12, we find very similar elements, arranged differently: there is the attestation of Scripture (particularly, the prophets), the key events of Christ's sufferings and subsequent glory, the interpretation that these are salvific, and mention of the fact that this "gospel" has been announced by others.

In Hebrews, somewhat similar elements are found at the outset of the letter (1:1–4), though in quite different language: God's public announcement in his Son is related to his previous speech in the prophets. This Son is said to have made purification for sins (later shown to occur in his sacrificial death), and then to

---

[15] A classic is C. H. Dodd, *The Apostolic Preaching and Its Developments* (London: Hodder & Stoughton, 1936).

[16] See the critiques in chapter 1 of Benjamin A. Edsall, *Paul's Witness to Formative Early Christian Instruction*, Wissenschaftliche Untersuchungen Zum Neuen Testament series, vol. 2 (Tübingen: Mohr Siebeck, 2014).

[17] See further my chapters "Kerygmatic Rhetoric in New Testament Epistles," in Stanley E. Porter and Matthew R. Malcolm, *Horizons in Hermeneutics* (see chap. 3, n. 37); "Biblical Hermeneutics and *Kerygmatic* Responsibility," in Stanley E. Porter and Matthew R. Malcolm, *The Future of Biblical Interpretation* (see chap. 4, n. 18; and "'He Interpreted to Them the Things about Himself in All the Scriptures': Linguistic Perspectives on the New Testament's Use of the Old Testament," coauthored with Ian G. Malcolm, in Matthew R. Malcolm, ed., *All That the Prophets Have Declared: The Appropriation of Scripture in the Emergence of Christianity* (Milton Keynes, UK: Paternoster, 2015).

have taken his place at the right hand of God in risen vindication. The rest of the letter flows from this important prelude.

In 1 John, we find a very different voice: the circling rhetorical mode of the letter resists singular summaries. In place of the use of "gospel" as a key term for the Christian message, we find the Johannine "testimony," and although Old Testament themes are clearly utilized, there is little explicit reflection on the attesting role of Old Testament prophets. Nevertheless, the salvific work of God in the Son remains crucial, bringing forgiveness for sin (4:10) and new life: "And this is the testimony: God has given us eternal life, and this life is in his Son" (5:11).

In James, a condensed "gospel" summary is also lacking. But we do find that belief in the "glorious Lord Jesus Christ" (2:1) ought to result in an identification with the suffering poor, who are heirs of the kingdom (2:5), rather than the exploitative rich, who are destined for destruction. These rich are the ones who "condemned" and "murdered" the righteous one (5:6). Why is this identification fitting for those who believe in the "glorious Lord Jesus Christ"? Presumably because this belief entails the key convictions that Jesus condescended to suffer unjustly and received glorified vindication in God's timing.

All of these New Testament passages, from a variety of writers, resound with the major hermeneutical impact assigned to Jesus himself in Luke's Gospel. In Luke 24, the risen Jesus insists that "all the Scriptures" testify to his suffering and resurrected glory. They are events that secure "forgiveness of sins" and must be announced to all nations (vv. 27, 47). This ought to be carefully noted: according to Jesus here, the whole of the Old Testament testifies to the elements that are elsewhere called "gospel."

It remains arguable, then, that the different voices of the canon may be heard in the light of this key theme. But in contrast with some scholarship of the early twentieth century, it has become crucial in scholarship of this century to give due justice to the distinctive "voice" (to use Bakhtin's imagery) of each New Testament contribution, and not to be too quick to offer surface harmonization. Benjamin Edsall, a postdoctoral research fellow in the Institute for Religion and Critical Inquiry, argued,

> If one is to attend to the question of the content of early Christian teaching and preaching, as I contend one should, certain lessons from previous attempts must be taken to heart. Form criticism, with its attendant synthetic approach across a number of texts, is too problematic a basis for reconstructing anything other than a general pastiche of recurrent early Christian themes. A new approach must treat texts as whole cloth, attending to their rhetoric and supplying a nuanced view of their

referential value. Further, mining the speeches in Acts for the earliest Christian preaching is problematic in light of their literary function and context. And, finally, one must not start with the determinative presupposition of a unified early church.[18]

The earliest "cloths" in the fabric of the New Testament are, as Edsall went on to point out, the letters of Paul. A number of works have indeed attempted to be attentive to the nature of Paul's "gospel," or teaching in particular, and its relation to his own hermeneutical stance.

Gospel in Paul

Edsall himself shies away from the term *kerygma*, finding it too "plastic" due to its association with form criticism. Nevertheless, he discerns that Paul's own witness to his formational church teaching suggests that he did teach, and assumed that others taught, key elements of a "Christ-centered, monotheistic symbolic universe":[19]

> In both cities [Corinth and Thessalonica] Paul taught about God as the one true God the father (both of Jesus and of believers), Jesus as Christ and Lord who died "for us," was raised by God and will come again imminently as judge . . . The Holy Spirit featured in Paul's formative instruction as accompanying his preaching, a gift to the believers from God and itself a bestower of gifts such as prophecy and glossolalia. According to Paul, he preached his gospel as an apostle and without sophistry.[20]

Edsall compares these features with the elements that Paul assumed were known and embraced by the Roman church—a church he did not plant. He finds that each element involves some continuity and discontinuity. Paul appeared to expect that other Christian teachers had laid common foundations regarding God as the Father of the dead-and-risen Lord Jesus Christ, belief and baptism in Christ, the work of the Spirit, and the impetus for moral transformation. But Paul seemed to infer that some of the mechanics and details of these things the Romans had not understood in a Pauline sense.

---

[18] Edsall, *Paul's Witness to Formative Early Christian Instruction*, 12.

[19] Ibid., 174.

[20] Ibid., 170.

In Matthew W. Bates's analysis of Paul's interpretive instincts, he is happier to use the descriptive term *kerygmatic*, using it to encapsulate the vantage point from which Paul considers the Scriptures.[21] He summarized his approach:

> Paul received, utilized, and extended an apostolic, kerygmatic narrative tradition centered on key events in the Christ story as his primary interpretative lens—a narrative tradition that already contained a built-in hermeneutic . . . In short, the received apostolic proclamation acts as a 'center' for Paul, giving fundamental hermeneutical guidance as it operates within his larger notion of a divine economy.[22]

The key "christocentric narrative sequences"[23] that characterize Paul's kerygmatic hermeneutic are crystallized in 1 Cor 15:3–5, in which (as we saw earlier) Christ is portrayed as having died for sins in accordance with Scripture, been buried, been raised on the third day in accordance with Scripture, and appeared to Cephas and the Twelve. Bates has pointed out that in holding to the primacy and hermeneutical significance of these convictions, Paul was in continuity with other apostolic teachers: "Paul's rhetorical use of 1 Corinthians 15:3b–5 in 1 Corinthians 15 demands that Paul himself accepted the protocreed in its entirety, including the normativeness of its hermeneutical statements. It is necessary to stress emphatically this point, since there is a tendency in some quarters to argue for a hermeneutical disjuncture between Paul and the pre-Pauline tradition he cites."[24]

In my own work on Paul as a letter-writer in 1 Corinthians,[25] I suggest that Paul's *kerygma*, which I take to be focused on Christ's death and risen exaltation—as informed by the Jewish motif of reversal—impacted both Paul's conceptualization of issues in Corinth and the rhetorical shape of his response. Thus, Paul's gospel both draws on and interprets the Old Testament Scriptures, as well as directing Paul's apostolic ministry.

---

[21] Note that New Testament scholar Richard Hays uses similar concepts: "A Gospel-shaped hermeneutic necessarily entails *reading backwards*, reinterpreting Israel's Scripture in light of the story of Jesus." Richard B. Hays, *Reading Backwards: Figural Christology and the Fourfold Gospel Witness* (Waco: Baylor University Press, 2014), 104.

[22] Matthew W. Bates, *The Hermeneutics of the Apostolic Proclamation: The Center of Paul's Method of Scriptural Interpretation* (Waco: Baylor University Press, 2012), 56–57.

[23] Ibid., 60.

[24] Ibid., 64.

[25] Matthew R. Malcolm, *Paul and the Rhetoric of Reversal in 1 Corinthians: The Impact of Paul's Gospel on his Macro-Rhetoric*, Society for New Testament Studies Monograph Series (Cambridge: Cambridge University Press, 2013).

This attention to Paul's own gospel (Rom 2:16) will no doubt be fruitful for the sort of project Edsall described, of attempting to give adequate attention to each "voice" (Bakhtin) or "cloth" (Edsall) that makes up the New Testament polyphony/fabric. At the same time, it should be remembered, as noted earlier, that Paul believed that "whether . . . it [was] I or they, [this is what] we proclaim[ed]" (1 Cor 15:11; cf. Rom 6:17; Col 1:23). Thus, it is not out of place, while the project continues, to hold provisionally to the traditional Christian conviction that the "good news" regarding Jesus's death and resurrection as Messiah of Israel and Lord of all is declared in all the Scriptures.

Graeme Goldsworthy reflected:

> We can say that, while not all Scripture is the gospel, all Scripture is related to the gospel that is its center . . .
>
> For the student of the Bible, the gospel becomes the norm by which the whole Old Testament and all the exhortations and other non-gospel aspects of the New Testament are to be understood.[26]

Gospel and the Whole Bible

If this is so, then a consideration of "gospel" necessarily leads to a consideration of "biblical theology" of some sort. Goldsworthy commented, "The fact that the prophetic word of the Old Testament leads to the incarnate Word, who is the explicit subject of the New Testament (Heb. 1:1–2), means that we examine and take on board the evidence for the relationship of all Scripture to Christ. The dynamic of biblical theology demands a sound theological exegesis that is the heart of our movement from text to hearer."[27]

The term "biblical theology" is not always used in the same way. For some it means theology that is drawn from the Bible; for others it means theology that represents common themes throughout the breadth of the Bible; for others (like Goldsworthy, as seen previously) it means the canon's unfolding witness to the gospel of Jesus Christ, who is himself the Bible's theological center point. It is this sense that interests us here.

---

[26] Goldsworthy, *Gospel-Centred Hermeneutics*, 63 (see chap. 4, n. 6).
[27] Ibid., 201.

> Biblical theology *is an approach to the Bible that hears in the documents of the Old and New Testaments a richly concordant unfolding revelation of divine salvation that comes to a climax in the person and work of Jesus Christ, as expressed in the gospel. This approach arises both from the eschatological and intertextual impulses of the documents themselves, and the theological conviction that the Scriptures are a divinely given unity.*

While it has been expressed in a variety of ways, it is clear that the impulse to view the Bible as a whole as God's unfolding revelatory witness to his Son has been a persistent feature among Christian interpreters. We noted in chapter 4 that this hermeneutical impulse has been combined with a great diversity of interpretive methods in different instances, including allegory, typology, "plain" readings, "law/gospel" readings, historical-critical methodologies, and so on—resulting in a diversity of interpretive outcomes. Nevertheless, the impulse itself would seem to be a fairly ubiquitous component of historic Christian interpretation. Whether Irenaeus, Augustine, Bede, Aquinas, Angela of Foligno, Luther, Calvin, Spurgeon, or today's Christian churches is in view, it is a feature of Christian interpretation that the Christian Bible is about Christ.

But given these different interpretive applications, how can we properly apply this impulse that the gospel of Jesus Christ relates to all of Scripture? We will consider this issue especially in chapter 10, when we look at interpreting the Old Testament as Christian Scripture. At this point, it is enough to note that it is an appropriate "instinct" for Christian interpretation.

These three major elements, then—theology, canon, and gospel—will be fruitful parts of primed pre-understanding in approaching the Bible as Christian Scripture.

BIG IDEA

A defining characteristic of Christian interpretation is that interpreters consider the biblical documents to be in the realm of Christian Scripture. This entails approaching them with a pre-understanding shaped by the refined heritage of systematic theology, recognizing the parameters and potential connections set by the canon, and the cohering center of the gospel of Jesus Christ.

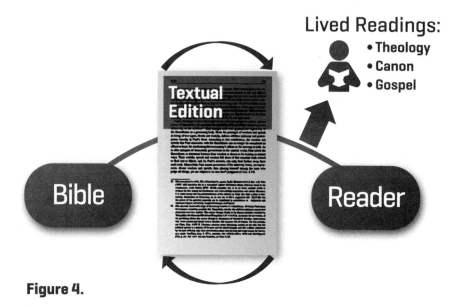

Figure 4.

Questions for Discussion

1. How can we hold together the concepts of *unity* and genuine *polyphony* in the Bible?

2. What are the benefits and dangers of holding to a heritage of systematic theology when approaching the Bible for exegesis?

3. Consider a specific passage of the Bible that is of interest to you. How will an acknowledgment of the context of the canon impact the way this passage is interpreted?

4. What is the gospel according to Paul? Is this the same gospel as that attested by Mark? By John? By Peter?

5. How might a conviction that the Bible centers on the gospel impact the way the Old Testament is interpreted?

For Further Reading

Goldsworthy, Graeme. 2012. *Christ-Centered Biblical Theology: Hermeneutical Foundations and Principles.* Downers Grove, IL: IVP Academic.———. 2007. *Gospel-Centered Hermeneutics: Foundations and Principles of Evangelical Biblical Interpretation.* Downers Grove, IL: IVP Academic.

8

FROM HERMENEUTICS TO EXEGESIS: PRIMING AND REFINING

At this point we will move to focus more deliberately on the process of interpreting biblical passages. This will draw together all that we have seen so far, and will become quite practical.

Interviewing the Bible

We have seen that different texts might be said to be on a spectrum, from more open (e.g., haiku) to more closed (e.g., an instruction manual). The Bible contains texts with elements from both ends of the spectrum, as well as much in between. I have suggested that to read such texts responsibly, it is wise to think of the interpretive task as being somewhat like an interview process, rather than a singular method.

Applying this to exegesis will involve both *priming* (that is, pre-interview homework) and *refining* (that is, continually cultivating one's general sense of the text by asking particular questions of it). While it is the refining stage that is most properly referred to as "exegesis," the priming stage is essential for the self-aware

Consider the best interviews you have seen. For me, the most gripping interviews are conducted by visibly involved people, rather than those sticking to rigid sets of questions. I still remember seeing a television interview years ago in which the reporter was questioning a political figure who had divisive views on race. I remember the heat in the interviewer's face when he said that he himself was of racially mixed parentage. This engagement between the figures on the screen made for a fascinating and unpredictable interview. If we want to engage effectively with texts (or other people), we would do well to celebrate the fact that we are real people, rather than seeking to become objectively robotic.

interpreter. I should point out, though, that even before embarking on priming for exegesis, I would want to read through the text in question for pleasure, allowing it to impact me as it will. Following this initial "aesthetic" reading, I would move on to the stages that follow.

Priming

We need to recognize immediately that the point of doing this pre-interview homework is not to expose every facet of our preliminary understanding so that we can approach the text with full knowledge. That would be impossible: we cannot exhaust an understanding of the text's context, and we are not even aware of many facets of our own makeup. Even as we seek to consider facets of the contexts that impact our texts and ourselves, we are already making use of faculties that exist in particularly shaped parameters of time and space. There is no such thing as fully self-aware investigation. Nevertheless, some attention to the locatedness of our texts and ourselves will be an important part of preparing to engage seriously with them.

These matters of priming occur instinctively in many instances of normal communication, and it would be tedious to start from scratch with their investigation in every act of exegesis. However, exegesis is by its nature a task that involves examining, analyzing, and questioning elements that would otherwise be assumed, or grasped instinctively, or perhaps missed entirely. So, these matters are worth bringing into conscious focus at the outset of the exegetical examination of a particular book of the Bible, even if they need not be repeatedly rehearsed in reading each new passage.

Initial priming for a biblical book might profitably pay attention to the four dimensions of contextual locatedness that we have seen already: *realm*, *mission*, *emergence*, and *reception*, as follows.

The Bible's Realm

My provisional understanding (arising, as a Christian interpreter, from the "refined" insights of systematic theology) is that the Old Testament opens, and the New Testament completes, the Christian biblical canon, as the Word of God. (However, I can also posit other realms and engage with the realms applied by others.) I will therefore always want to ask something along these lines: *Are there ways in which this book carries important connections with other parts of the biblical canon?*

In a particular instance of priming for exegetical work on the books of Kings, I might ask: Does this book draw on God's promises to Abraham, and/or God's promises to David? How does it pave the way for the coming of Jesus? In an instance of priming for exegetical work on 1 Peter, I might ask: Does this book draw on prophetic hope? If so, how? Does it utilize Old Testament imagery? What images are important?

The Bible's Mission

My provisional/refined stance is that the Old Testament arises from writers who believed they were writing or speaking into God's history for Israel, and the New Testament arises from apostolic mission, in summoning people to God together through the gospel of Jesus's death and exaltation as Messiah of Israel and Lord of all. So, for an Old Testament book, I will always want to ask questions such as: *How does this book tell or speak into redemptive history? What is affirmed about God's dealings with Israel? What is left in question?* For a New Testament book, I will always want to ask questions such as: *How does this book form part of the apostolic missionary strategy? Is it for the upbuilding of disciples? Is it for evangelism?*

For example, when preparing to conduct exegetical work on the Old Testament book of Jonah, I might ask: Why does this book exist? What was it saying to Israel that Israel needed to hear? And why did Israel need to hear it? When preparing to do exegesis on the epistle to the Hebrews, I might ask: Does this book reiterate the gospel to encourage waning believers to persevere? Does it arise from the Pauline wing of early Christian mission (even if not by Paul himself)? If so, how would an understanding of the Pauline mission illuminate the letter?

The Bible's Emergence

At the same time, the Bible consists of human literary products that emerged in particular instances of space, time, and language. To various degrees, one can determine geographical, historical, social, and literary contexts for the various books of the Bible. I will therefore always want to ask something along these lines: *What are the general locations, times, movements, and language issues relevant for this book?*

When looking into the book of Genesis, I will want to look at maps that show the travels of the patriarchs. When looking into the book of Deuteronomy, I might ask: Is there weight to the claim that ancient suzerainty treaties illuminate the progression of this book? When looking into the Gospels, I might ask: Who were the Pharisees? Who was Herod? When looking into the book of Acts, I might ask: Why do people say that Luke's Greek is superior to that of certain other New Testament authors? How can I best understand his use of language?

The Bible's Reception

The Bible has been mediated to us through two millennia of tradition and interpretation. Certain lines of interpretation have become stabilized, while other elements have been highly contested. Some passages of Scripture have had enormous cultural impacts, while others appear to have gone largely unnoticed. Some have been prized in certain cultural settings but not in others. I will therefore always want to ask something along these lines: *What impact has this book had across history? How has it been regarded and used?*

For example, in preparing for exegesis on the book of Judges, I might ask: How did early Judaism interpret this book? How has subsequent Judaism interpreted the book? How did the Christian patristics interpret this book? In preparing for exegesis on the New Testament book of 2 Corinthians, I might ask: What do we know about the ongoing experience of the Corinthian church after this letter? Does Clement's epistle to the Corinthians (c. 96) illuminate how the letter might have been received? Why have some scholars viewed this letter as a redaction of multiple letters? When and why did this view come into prominence? Have others, in different ages or cultures, had similar difficulties with the abrupt changes in the letter?

My Realm

At the same time, we want to consider different facets of our own locatedness as interpreters. However, it will be crucial for me to recognize that I am by no means conscious of all that makes up me. I will therefore need to accompany this attempted self-awareness with self-critical humility.

The very mention of "conscious" or "unconscious" self-understanding perhaps reminds of Freudian psychoanalysis, which brought these concepts into the Western worldview. Apart from Ricoeur's critical interaction with Freud, the field of hermeneutics has had surprisingly little to do with psychoanalytical thought, despite its keen insistence that interpreters are not conscious of all that they bring to a hermeneutical encounter.[1] However, psychoanalysis has moved on since Freud, and in very interesting directions. For example, H. J. Home argued in the 1960s that psychoanalysis itself should be thought of as a hermeneutical practice within the humanities, rather than a pseudoscientific pursuit.[2] Present psychoanalytic

---

[1]   I am very grateful to Dr. Jim Crawley for his help on these matters. Crawley is a private practitioner of psychoanalytic psychotherapy and was the inaugural president of the Psychotherapy and Counselling Federation of Australia. I draw on his expertise in this paragraph.

[2]   H. J. Home, "The Concept of Mind," *International Journal of Psychoanalysis* 47 (1966): 42–49.

theory emphasizes features such as the impact of past (especially unconscious) experience on present interpretation; the value of empathic attunement on the part of an analyst; and the priority of understanding over explanation. It may well be that this will become an area of fruitful engagement between disciplines in the future.

With an awareness that caution and humility are required, then, it can be valuable for the interpreter to consider his or her own identity and reflect on what the interviewer might be bringing—consciously or not—to the interview. I will always want to ask, in a general way, therefore, *Are there ways that my identity or my past might attune me or blind me to elements of the text?*

For instance, I am Matthew Malcolm—with all that that entails. In part, it means that I am a married, white, Australian male working in a Christian, government-accredited Indonesian university. How might any of these elements impact my reading of the text? How will my particular struggles impact my reading of texts in which those struggles are triggered? How will my particular desires or frustrations or hopes or disappointments impact how I hear the Bible?

My Reading Mission

Everyone who reads a text has some reason for doing so, whether to gain information, or to derive pleasure; to avoid trouble, or to alleviate boredom; to seek change, to find a loophole, or to grow as a person. It is important to try to be honest about the question, for what purpose am I interpreting the Bible? For some, the answer might be that they want to grow as disciples; for others, perhaps they want to contradict existing traditions; for others still, it might be for ministry purposes. It is worth trying to be up front in facing the question: *Are there ways that my intentions might attune me or blind me to elements of the text?*

For example, the late Helmut Koester, of Harvard Divinity School, wrote, "Interpretation of the Bible is justified only if it is a source for political and religious renewal, or it is not worth the effort."[3] How would this reading mission impact his interpretation of the text? How will *my* reading mission(s) impact my interpretation of the text?

My Emergence

Everyone comes from somewhere, and almost everyone can identify his or her main language. This does not mean that the identification of cultural and linguistic

---

[3] Helmut Koester, "Epilogue: Current Issues in New Testament Scholarship," in Birger A. Pearson, ed., *The Future of Early Christianity: Essays in Honor of Helmut Koester* (Minneapolis: Fortress Press, 1991), 475.

issues is simple; it can be exceedingly complex! Nevertheless, it is worth spending some time considering the question: How would I describe my culture(s) and language(s)? *Further, are there elements of my language or culture that might attune or blind me to elements of the text?*

For example, the English language does not distinguish grammatically between second person singular and plural. How might this impact my assumptions when I read the text? Australian culture (in which I grew up) does not have an important place for ritual cleanness and uncleanness. How might this impact the way I hear the text? What can I learn from the impact this text has in Indonesian culture (where I live), or from readers who are located differently from myself?

My Reception Community

Most people who read the Bible do so within traditions and communities—whether ecclesial, academic, familial, or online—that nurture them as interpreters. These need not be denied or bracketed out when entering into exegesis, but it will be fruitful to acknowledge them and consider their legacies. It will be useful to ask this question: *Are there ways that my reading traditions or communities might attune or blind me to elements of the text?*

For some, answers will come fairly clearly. The way they examine Bible text will be influenced by a reading tradition that is mainly Southern Baptist, Evangelical Anglican, Wesleyan, Nicene, Marxist, secular, etc. For others, it will take some time to consider the traditions or communities that have offered nurture. We may be optimistic that a thoughtful Christian tradition will ground readers in faithful prejudices as they approach Christian texts. Nevertheless, we should be aware of other reading communities than our own, which may bring with them different attunements.

Having primed ourselves by considering these features of the *horizon of the text* and the *horizon of the reader*, we come to the task of exegesis itself, which is essentially a process of refining questioning.

Refining

With a conscious awareness of the issues raised in the pre-interview locational facets of *realm, mission, emergence,* and *reception,* we might approach passages of interest with a "refining" interview process. This productive hermeneutical circle involves a movement from general, through particular, back out toward a refined general sense.

> Exegesis *involves a consciously located interpreter (or community of interpreters) questioning a particular text, in thoughtful awareness of dimensions of locatedness of the biblical other. This questioning aims to result in rigorous, respectful interpretation of a particular written text. Sometimes this term is used specifically to refer to interpretation of biblical texts in the original languages.*

The General: Approaching the Text

The exegete begins by discerning a *provisional big picture or impact* of the book and then the passage concerned in context. This might involve the following:

At the level of the whole book . . .

- considering its initial aesthetic impact
- recalling the pertinent areas of priming
- developing one's own "map" or literary structure of the book as a whole
- reading an introduction or exposition of the book as a whole
- hearing how a "fan" or devotee characterizes or summarizes the book

At the level of a specific passage . . .

- considering the literary context of the passage in focus
- reading the passage in English and evaluating its initial aesthetic impact
- identifying the "big idea" of the passage
- considering questions provoked by the initial reading, including personal and theological challenges

The Particular: Observing the Text

Coming to the level of the particular, the exegete moves to *observing the text*, analyzing such things as syntax, backgrounds, and rhetoric. *This is the bulk of exegetical work* and might involve asking *who, what, where, when, why,* and *how* questions regarding the language choices evident in the text. It may involve . . .

- moving slowly through the text, asking how the elements of each clause function and relate to one another
- asking text-critical questions
- asking about the meanings of words in their contexts and relationships
- asking about relevant backgrounds of topics/motifs/places/names/historical details
- asking about larger-scale connections

- asking why things are expressed in the way that they are, and considering the active impacts of the passage on its initial hearers
- asking how others have understood or been impacted by the passage (particularly in other ages and cultures)

This is an inquisitive analysis of the content of the text, primed with an appreciation for issues of locatedness and informed by an understanding of relevant linguistic issues. I will give more detailed attention to linguistic issues later in this chapter.

Back to the General: Interacting with the Text

From here the exegete begins to move toward the general again, refining his or her prior sense of the passage (and the whole book) by consciously *interacting with the text*. Having observed the particulars of the text in some detail, the exegete is now prepared to reengage his or her provisional sense of the passage in an informed way. This may be both more personal and more integrative, and it might involve . . .

- drawing together the big picture and impacts of the passage
- engaging further with alternative readings of the passage, from other locations
- asking how the text might speak into my/our situation today—in particular, asking how this passage calls me and my ecclesial community to be transformed, or to transform the world

Linguistic Issues in Exegesis

The level of the "particular," referenced earlier, needs some further elucidation, particularly for those using the original languages. We noted in our chapter on hermeneutical foundations that dialogue occurs *in language*, so even those who are not using Hebrew and Greek can benefit from a basic understanding of how language operates. More comprehensive guides can be found elsewhere.[4]

We have seen already (in our discussion of Augustine and in our discussion of general foundations) that language expresses mental representations of reality in

---

[4] Aside from reference grammars on the biblical languages, see the following introductory books: Peter James Silzer and Thomas John Finley, *How Biblical Languages Work: A Student's Guide to Learning Hebrew and Greek* (Grand Rapids: Kregel, 2004); and David Alan Black, *Linguistics for Students of New Testament Greek: A Survey of Basic Concepts and Applications*, 2nd ed. (Grand Rapids: Baker, 1988, 1995).

signs.[5] These linguistic signs can be analyzed in terms of their form and function. Elements of such analysis that are particularly relevant for biblical exegesis would include *morphology, syntax, semantics,* and *pragmatics*. These categories overlap but can be distinguished. Our examination of them here will necessarily be brief and introductory.

Morphology

> Morphology *refers to the forms, and changes of form, that words can take in order to communicate different sorts of meaning.*

In the English words *they saw*, we see a third person plural past-tense construction, which is different from the third person singular future, *she will see*. Articulating the morphological distinction between the verbs *saw* and *will see* involves a more particular scrutiny than is normally needed in day-to-day conversation, but it allows analytical precision. In terms of nouns, there is a morphological distinction between the singular *book* and the plural *books*. This is seen in the affixed morpheme *s*. In a different instance, the change works differently: *shelf* becomes *shelves*. And from this noun we derive a related verb: to *shelve* a project. Thus there are both *inflectional* and *derivational* morphemes.

The exegete who is working with original languages will need to pay careful attention to the forms of the words in the text. Hebrew and Greek morphology need to be understood and applied so that the exegete can articulate that *miqvaot* is a feminine plural noun, or *anabaineis* is a second person singular present verb.

Pokorný points, however, to "an important rule of exegesis: the basic *bearer of meaning is not the word alone, but the sentence*."[6] That does not mean that words are unimportant, but rather that they should be seen properly for what they are. As Pokorný goes on to say, "A lexeme, in the basic sense in which this term is used, is a word in all its grammatical (morphological) forms and syntactic (grammatical and stylistic) connections—that is, a word as a phenomenon."[7]

This brings us to a consideration of syntax.

---

[5] Charles K. Ogden and I. A. Richards saw this as a triangle. To use Moisés Silva's adjustment of their terminology, the reality is the *referent*, the sign is the *symbol*, and the mental representation is the *sense*. Cited in Constantine Campbell, *Advances in the Study of Greek: New Insights for Reading the New Testament* (Grand Rapids: Zondervan, 2015), 73.

[6] Pokorný, *Hermeneutics as a Theory of Understanding*, 19; emphasis in original (see chap. 6, n. 3).

[7] Ibid., 22–23.

Syntax

> Syntax *refers to how words can meaningfully come together. Words are combined in phrases and clauses, which function in relation to one another in order to communicate.*

Taking some of the words used in the preceding discussion of morphology, we could create the clause "You do not, in fact, see books on the top shelf." Given the word order, we see that the subject is the pronoun *you*, and that the present *seeing* is negated. The plural object, *books*, is related to a further object, which is qualified by an adjective: *top* shelf. Furthermore, the natural reader will detect that there is some surprise in the negation, flagged by the interruption of the words *in fact*.

The reader of Old Testament Hebrew will need to recognize that the words *bara Elohim et hashamayim* follow the default Hebrew word order of verb-subject-object: "created God the heaven" (though of course we would not translate it in this order). The reader of New Testament Greek will need to recognize that in the clause *theos ēn ho logos* (John 1:1), the subject is *ho logos* (because it has the article), and the predicate is *theos*. Thus we understand it to mean, "the word was God," rather than "God was the word." These are matters of syntax—rightly discerning relationships between words.

Connections occur not only between words, but also between phrases, clauses, and paragraphs, extending to the level of a whole discourse.

But what if, after being told, "You do not, in fact, see books on the top shelf," you were to respond, "I see"? Are you acknowledging, or disagreeing with, what you had just been told? This brings us to consider semantics and pragmatics. Again, remember that these categories overlap—but we will be distinguishing them here for the sake of simplicity and clarity.

Semantics

> Semantics *refers to the meaning that is communicated by words both individually and in syntactic context.*

Sometimes English users say "see" when they refer to sight, and sometimes they say "see" when they refer to understanding. The same word can have different meanings in different contexts (and will usually take only one particular meaning in each context).

We have seen already that much use of language is metaphorical—especially when used for abstract concepts. The exegete will need to work out what the context suggests. When someone responds to the statement about the empty top shelf with the words, "I see," he or she is *probably* using the term in the metaphorical sense of *understanding* (particularly because "I see" is a standard speech act expressing concurrence); although the context would not rule out the literal sense of meaning: "My vision of the top shelf tells me that what you say is true." It is unlikely that the person would mean "But I *do* see the books," because we would expect such a stark contradiction to be expressed with a more emphatic construction.

Semantic features may be common to a number of words, in a particular respect: *see, fathom, conceive,* and *appreciate* can all share the semantic feature *understand,* but also carry other semantic features that are not related.

Let us imagine that our interlocutor responds to the statement about the shelf by nodding toward a lone book at the far end of the top shelf and saying, "Oh, I . . . *see!*" We perceive that the attention-grabbing effect of the "Oh," the pause after the "I," and the emphatic "*see*" draw attention to the fact that this is supposed to be heard in an ironic way (employing a pun on two senses of "see"). But to understand what is going on, we want to push further: Is this ironic statement an act of aggression, subversion, or jocularity?

Or consider another scenario: what if our interlocutor is a non-native English speaker and replies to the statement about the top shelf, saying, "Oh, I . . . *see!*" Would we still take this as ironic? Would we still take it as metaphorical? This brings us to consider pragmatics.

Pragmatics

> Pragmatics *concerns the ways the purposes for using language are actualized in sociocultural settings.*

Language choices are made by particularly located people, whose mental representations of reality are culturally shaped and who operate in situations of social interaction. Remember: "knowing what words and sentences mean is one thing: knowing what *people* mean is another."[8]

How might this impact exegesis of the Bible? It means, at least, that the existence of a real-life author, however hard to precisely identify, remains relevant. In relation to *cultural shaping,* I have commented elsewhere on the significance of the fact that Paul, who wrote in Greek, was a self-confessed "Hebrew of Hebrews":

> In seeking to be attentive to the arrangement of Paul's communication it is necessary to move beyond the examination of *genre* (or *form,* or

---

[8] Ian G. Malcolm, "Pragmatics," 4 (see chap. 5, n. 30).

rhetorical convention), to consider broader issues of flexible *mental imagery* and *cultural conceptualisation*. Additionally, it is necessary to move beyond the practical assumption of a monolithic Greco-Roman rhetorical culture, to emphasise, within the complexity of Paul's identity and literary manner, the significant influence of his *kerygma* "in accordance with the Scriptures." Just as it would be naïve to think that early Christianity, Judaism and Hellenism are completely separable, it would also be naïve to think that the interpretative and communicative motifs of Judaism—or of the Messianic sect to which Paul was converted—were effectively dissolved in the conventions of Greco-Roman oratory.[9]

In other words, Paul was not a generic letter-writer, but a *particular* person. If we are to understand him, we should pay attention to his particularity.

In relation to the exegetical significance of *social interaction*, we might consider Paul's comment to the Corinthians in 1 Corinthians 15:1 (my translation): "Now I inform you, brothers and sisters, of the gospel that I proclaimed to you . . ." An analysis of morphology and syntax allows this translation. But consider the social context of this comment. It occurs in a highly charged relationship, in which the Corinthian Christians are judging Paul against other leaders and considering him to be inferior to their own heights of spiritual discernment. In fact, just four verses before this point, Paul acknowledges that some in Corinth think themselves to be "prophets" or "spiritual." In this charged social atmosphere, Paul decides to "remind" them of, or "make known" to them the basics of the gospel. This is no calm reminder, but a confronting act of subversion. To miss this is to fail to capture the full meaning of the passage, which transcends morphological and syntactic analysis.

Writing an Exegesis Paper

At times there will be a need to produce an "exegesis paper" based on a particular passage of the Bible. This sort of work especially aims to consider, from the reader's vantage point, the burden of the text in its original contexts. Rather than

BIG IDEA

Exegesis involves a consciously located interpreter (or community of interpreters) questioning a particular text, in thoughtful awareness of dimensions of locatedness of the biblical other. Hermeneutically informed biblical exegesis could fruitfully build on initial "priming" in the areas of realm, mission, emergence, and reception, with linguistically careful "refining" questioning of a particular text. An "exegesis paper" will demonstrate the outcomes of this exegesis.

---

[9] Matthew R. Malcolm, *Paul and the Rhetoric of Reversal*, 31.

being "live" exegesis or interpretation, such a paper captures the *outcomes* of exegesis. It therefore should not take the form of questions, but of clearly argued findings that have resulted from one's interpretive questioning. The following would be a reasonable way of putting the refining exegetical values of this chapter into a clear structure for such a paper:

Approaching the text:

- Recall any pertinent areas of general priming and demonstrate the literary context of the passage.
- Give a provisional big idea of the passage.
- Flag any obvious questions provoked by the passage.
- Consider the structure of the passage.

- 20% of paper

Observing the text:

- Move slowly through the text, giving linguistically informed analysis of how the elements function and relate to one another.
- Deal with text-critical questions for the passage.
- Comment on the contextual meanings of relevant (e.g., disputed/ambiguous/major) words.
- Explain the relevance of any illuminating backgrounds of topics/motifs/places/names/historical details.
- Consider broad structure, macro-rhetoric, and larger-scale connections.
- Interact with how others have understood the passage (historically and today).
- Consider *why* things are expressed in the way that they are: what is the rhetorical force of the passage?

- 70% of paper

Interacting with the text:

- Draw some conclusions from the preceding observations.
- Consider again the big idea of the passage.
- Consider the significance of theology, canon, and gospel.
- Consider how you are impacted and how we should hear the burden of the text for today.

- 10% of paper

In subsequent chapters, we will consider some of the issues that come up when this sort of exegetical approach is applied to the Old and New Testaments. There will be a sample exegesis paper, using this structure, in chapter 11.

Questions for Discussion

1. If you were asked to interview the king of Thailand, how would you prepare? In what ways is this similar to or different from the sort of preparation that might help you be ready for exegesis?

2. What makes for good exegesis?

3. How would you explain morphology? Syntax? Semantics? Pragmatics?

4. What elements of the exegetical process outlined in this chapter come most naturally to you? What elements would take more conscious work to put into practice?

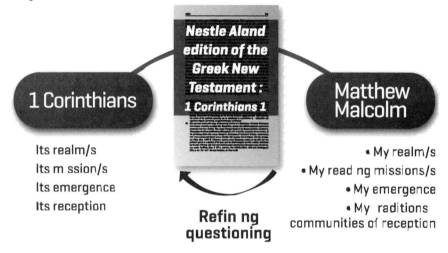

Figure 5.

For Further Reading

Carson, D. A. 1996. *Exegetical Fallacies.* Second edition. Grand Rapids: Baker Academic.

Duvall J. Scott, and J. Daniel Hays. 2012. *Grasping God's Word: A Hands-On Approach to Reading, Interpreting, and Applying the Bible.* Third Edition. Grand Rapids: Zondervan.

Hayes, John H., and Carl R. Holladay. 2007. *Biblical Exegesis: A Beginner's Handbook.* Third edition. Louisville: Westminster John Knox Press.

Gorman, Michael J. 2009. *Elements of Biblical Exegesis.* Grand Rapids: Baker Academic.

9

EXEGETICAL METHODS

Having developed a simple hermeneutical model and noting how exegesis might be conducted in the light of this model, we can now examine some of the methods that have been proposed and utilized for exegesis across the centuries.

Rationales for Methods

The application of our hermeneutical model to exegesis in the previous chapter involves an orientation of primed, inquisitive questioning. For that reason it remains—perhaps frustratingly—general and exploratory in tone. I am hesitant to promote an all-purpose, comprehensive method of interpretation that will work for all texts, because that would be to work against a genuine encounter of "others," which brings with it the potential for surprise and peculiarity. Not every New Testament passage will be greatly illuminated by an understanding of first-century Jewish or Roman culture. Not every text will be illuminated by an awareness of authorship. Not every passage will be quick to offer theological insights or applications. One text will be tremendously illuminated by attending to the insights of readers from cultures in which Christians are heavily persecuted, while another will be almost impenetrable without an understanding of the practices of its original recipients. One text will be relatively closed to multiple interpretations, while another will invite rich imaginative input of devotionally attuned hearers.

Hans-Georg Gadamer wrote, "Understanding is no method but rather a form of community among those who understand each other."[1]

Thiselton has pointed out that there is no singular interpretive "method" that can be appropriately applied to the breadth of Scripture's polyphony: "'Hermeneutics' is no one single thing, but a vast variety of interpretative strategies, each of which depends for its value and effectiveness on the nature of the text and the varied goals and situations of readers. Each strategy has its strengths and each has its limitations."[2]

A Variety of Strategies and Perspectives

The model of interpretation that we have been developing aims for a *transforming engagement* of other-located *horizons*, as the interpreter engages the *hermeneutical circle* through linguistically informed *refining questioning* of the text. Some of the exegetical methods that have developed over history are particularly aimed at exploring the "otherness" of the ancient text's horizon. Other methods attempt to explore dimensions of contemporary horizons. Others focus on strategies for giving linguistically informed attention to texts. It may be helpful, then, to consider strategies according to these (imprecise and overlapping) divisions:

- Tools to explore the author/text's horizon
- Reading perspectives to enrich or challenge the reader's horizon
- Resources with which to question the text

Tools to Explore the Author/Text's Horizon

One method that seeks to give weight to the divine intention behind the text of Scripture is the use of *allegory*. This was far more prevalent in earlier eras of church history than today, and we have encountered it already in our historical overview. Many early interpreters held that God was speaking the gospel in Scripture, drawing attention to his Son, and equipping the Son's followers for godly lives. Therefore, it was reasoned, interpreters might listen attentively for this divine voice in all parts of Scripture. Just as Paul had sensed a deeper significance in the Old Testament command to let the grinding ox eat the grain (1 Cor 9:9; 1 Tim 5:18), and a deeper significance in the relationship between the Old Testament figures of Sarah and Hagar (Gal 4:21–31), such interpreters find significance beneath

---

[1] Foreword in Grondin, *Introduction to Philosophical Hermeneutics*, x (see chap. 2, n. 30).
[2] Anthony C. Thiselton, "The Hermeneutics of Pastoral Theology: Ten Strategies for Reading Texts in Relation to Varied Reading-Situations" in *Thiselton on Hermeneutics*, 349 (see chap. 5, n. 38).

the surface of Scripture. Each element of a narrative portion of Scripture is said to represent a deeper spiritual reality. If the worst this approach can do is remind interpreters of the gospel, then perhaps it is not as dangerous as it is sometimes made out to be! On the other hand, if generalized divine intentions are made to drown out the particularity of individual passages, all of Scripture may seem bland and disempowered.

The critical analysis of texts in the light of the historical elements behind those texts also has a significant heritage. John Chrysostom began his series on 1 Corinthians by considering the history, geography, and society of first century Corinth: "As Corinth is now the first city of Greece, so of old it prided itself on many temporal advantages, and more than all the rest, on excess of wealth. And on this account one of the heathen writers entitled the place 'the rich.' For it lies on the isthmus of the Peloponnesus, and had great facilities for traffic. The city was also full of numerous orators, and philosophers."[3]

But an overwhelming interest in elements "behind" the text came with the rise of *historical criticism* in Enlightenment Europe. University of Oxford theologian Robert Morgan commented, "Historical criticism changes the focus from the texts themselves to their context or the history behind them, and the latter interest often involves a more negative critical attitude to the texts, its sources."[4]

Although the Enlightenment's naive sense of detached objectivity can no longer be entertained, a number of historical-critical methodologies are still fruitful, enabling considered attention to the contexts of the "other." The Gospels, for example, do not hide the fact that Morgan mentioned: they draw on *sources* (Luke 1:1–4). *Source criticism* is therefore the attempt to consider the pre-history of a text. As with *form criticism* (which seeks to discern places in which a text draws upon formal literary conventions) and *redaction criticism* (which seeks to discern editorial activity in a text), it considers how the canonical form(s) of a text came to be, through the discerning editorial use of previously existing materials or conventions.

But it is not just the pre-history of the text that is of interest, but its locatedness within particular historical settings. This includes the circumstances of the author(s), the occasion of the writing, the values of the initial readers' culture, and other such issues. For example, the books of Samuel refer to a king named

---

[3] John Chrysostom, "Introduction," in Philip Schaff, ed., *Nicene and Post-Nicene Fathers*, ser., vol 12, *Chrysostom: Homilies on the Epistles of Paul to the Corinthians* (Peabody, MA: Hendrickson, 1889), 1.

[4] Robert Morgan, "Biblical Hermeneutics and *Critical* Responsibility," in Porter and Malcolm, *Horizons in Hermeneutics*, 81 (see chap. 3, n. 37).

David: what can be known of the historical David? The epistles utilize references to "stewards" and "slaves" (1 Pet 4:10; Rom 6:6). What can be known about relevant first-century stewards and slaves? Paul spoke of his own relationship with the Corinthians. What can be known about the occasions of Paul writing letters to them? New Testament scholar James Dunn wrote, "To abstract a historical text, like a NT writing, from its historical context is like lifting a goldfish from its bowl and expecting it to still function as a goldfish. Any suggestion that a historical text has a life of its own, and can be understood wholly or sufficiently in its own terms, from within itself, opens the door to *eisegesis* of all sorts."[5]

Archaeological analysis attempts to consider the material contexts that illuminate the ancient world. Although most archaeological finds in biblical locations do not directly impact the interpretation of biblical passages, they contribute to our understanding of the societies in which and for which the biblical texts were written. From the smallest coin to the design of whole cities, we can learn about the customs and values of people in biblical times.

An example of why this might be useful for the exegete would be Paul's discussion of head coverings in 1 Corinthians: archaeology can show us examples of hairstyles and head coverings from the time, from which we can infer social conventions.

Social-scientific analysis considers how societies operate and how the social contexts of biblical documents might help us understand them better. This sort of analysis often makes use of social models that have been developed in fields such as anthropology or sociology and applies them to relevant ancient societies. Eckhard Schnabel's comments on economic features of Jewish society are illustrative:

> Jewish society could be divided into the upper class, the retainers of the upper class, and the lower class. The criteria for membership in the upper class was [*sic*] power by office, role, property or influence . . . In the first century A.D. the upper class consisted of the Herodian court and the aristocratic priestly families, from which the high priests were appointed . . . The retainers of the . . . upper class included the administrators of the courts of Herod I and his sons, the members of the Sanhedrin in Jerusalem, local magistrates; the lower echelons of the retainer group consisted of secretaries, administrators and managers of estates, the tax collectors (*publicani*), military officers, property managers, accountants, treasurers of cities, local judges, priests, wholesalers, travelling tradespeople . . . The

---

[5] James Dunn, "Biblical Hermeneutics and *Historical* Responsibility," in Porter and Malcolm, *Horizons in Hermeneutics*, 70.

lower class included everyone who did not participate in the privileges of, and was not employed by, the elites: peasants and fishers, farm workers and tenant farmers, day laborers and wage laborers, serfs and slaves, artisans and traders, small tradespeople and peddlers.[6]

The terminology Schnabel has used here ("retainers," etc.) is drawn from the social sciences. Such approaches can be illuminating, but can also have their drawbacks. Roland Deines, Emeritus Professor of New Testament at the University of Nottingham, cautions that urban models of poverty need to be applied with great care to first-century Galilee, both because first-century Galilean villages were very different from large cities such as Rome and also because social status is not measured by economic factors alone.[7]

Indeed, the nature of first-century Judaism, whether in Galilee, Jerusalem, or the Diaspora, has become a major interest more broadly in analysis of the Bible since the twentieth century. The *analysis of ancient texts* is a crucial part of developing understanding in this area.

Bart Ehrman commented, "Jesus's disciples were lower-class, illiterate peasants from remote rural areas of Galilee, where very few people could read, let alone write, and let alone create full-scale compositions."[8]

But is this true? How does Ehrman know that Jesus's disciples were like this? If he is mistaken (which I believe he is, to an extent), how would we provide a counterargument? To take another example, is it true that first-century Jews were gripped by "works righteousness" and a frustration over overwhelming sin, as previous generations of biblical interpreters have sometimes claimed? How would we give an informed answer to this question? Anglican theological scholar Richard Bauckham has commented on the usefulness of early Jewish literature in considering questions such as these: "Insofar as the context of Jesus, the early church, and the NT writings was Jewish, these [extracanonical] writings provide us with

---

[6] Eckhard Schnabel, *Early Christian Mission: Jesus and the Twelve* (Downers Grove, IL: IVP, 2004), 194.

[7] Roland Deines, "God or Mammon: The Danger of Wealth in the Jesus Tradition and in the Epistle of James," in Matthias Konradt und Esther Schläpfer, eds., *Anthropologie und Ethik im Frühjudentum und im Neuen Testament* (Tübingen: Mohr Siebeck, 2014), 327–85. Dr. Schnabel is Mary French Rockefeller Distinguished Professor of New Testament at Gordon Conwell Theological Seminary.

[8] Bart Ehrman, *How Jesus Became God: The Exaltation of a Jewish Preacher from Galilee* (New York: Harper One, 2014), 244.

most of what we know about that context (along with archaeological evidence and some references to Judaism and Jewish history in pagan literature)."[9]

One recent issue in the study of ancient Judaism and Christianity in the light of its material and literary environments has been the significance of *empire*. What did it mean for Jews or Christians to live and communicate in the shadow of Assyrian, or Babylonian, or Persian, or Greek, or Roman empire? Have we missed allusions or nuances in the literature? N. T. Wright wrote, "For someone steeped in the Jewish apocalyptic tradition, as Paul was, it would have been impossible to imagine that Rome was 'insignificant.'"[10]

Anathea E. Portier-Young of Duke Divinity School, has considered this Jewish apocalyptic tradition as attested in its literature: "Apocalypse answered the empire. The writers of the apocalypses countered hegemonic cosmologies, imperial spectacle, and false claims to power by articulating and promulgating an alternative vision of the world. They turned the symbols and values of the empire upside down and asserted the truth in the place of falsehood."[11]

While interpretations of the data are hotly debated (and I think the significance of empire has been overplayed), these methods of considering the Bible in the light of its textual pre-history and material, social, and literary contexts continue to be important and fruitful.

Reading Perspectives to Enrich or Challenge the Reader's Horizon

We have seen that the acknowledgment of the locatedness of the reader has been an important development in hermeneutics. Thus, in the twentieth century a number of new interpretive approaches began to emerge, sometimes attending to historical readings of the text, sometimes de-privileging established readings, and sometimes foregrounding the located identity of the interpreter.

Reception history, aesthetic of reception, and *Wirkungsgeschichte* are names given to approaches that give careful attention to the effects of a text across history, whether in interpretive commentary or broader cultural impact.

Numerous series of biblical commentaries are now giving exclusive attention to earlier periods of church history, such as the patristic period or the Reformation

---

[9] Richard Bauckham, "The Relevance of Extracanonical Jewish Texts to New Testament Study," in Joel B. Green, ed., *Hearing the New Testament: Strategies for Interpretation*, 2nd ed. (Grand Rapids: Eerdmans, 2010), 68.

[10] N.T. Wright, *Paul and the Faithfulness of God*, parts III and IV (London: SPCK, 2013), 1281.

[11] Anathea E. Portier-Young, *Apocalypse Against Empire: Theologies of Resistance in Early Judaism* (Grand Rapids: Eerdmans, 2011), 217.

period, in order to "make available the richness of the Church's classical tradition of interpretation."[12]

At the same time, numerous "contextual" commentaries are appearing, giving voice to a variety of present-day reading settings. In a review of one such work, I noted,

> The positive payoff of this approach is that it can offer new illumination of themes that might otherwise be missed or downplayed. The danger of this approach is . . . that it might simplify the nuanced "otherness" of the first-century context.
>
> As this volume illustrates, different cultures and reading situations will approach the texts with different instincts, suggesting a range of fresh readings to be tried.
>
> This approach seems to hold the most promise when a resonance between cultural horizons enables augmented sensitivity to features of the "other." It is most hazardous when the commitments of a reading context flatten first-century nuances.[13]

Postcolonial approaches intentionally aim to resist "colonizing" tendencies in interpreting the Bible, such as highlighting readings that reinforce the status quo in situations of power imbalance. M. W. Dube Shomanah, who has particular expertise in the use of the Bible in Africa, summarizes: "Postcolonial theories situate almost all reading and writing of the past three to four hundred years within the parameters of imperial and colonial currents of dominance and resistance, challenging all readers and writers to examine their practices for imperial and colonial currents of domination and suppression."[14]

Such currents of domination or suppression might include inattention to biblical interpretation conducted in non-European languages, using the Bible as an instrument of control, and appealing to the Bible as a justification for conquest of others' land. Contrasting reading practices are fostered, sometimes privileging liberation readings, readings by poor or nonacademic interpreters, or readings that consciously question Western power.

---

[12] Robert Louis Wilken, series preface in *1 Corinthians Interpreted by Early Christian Commentators*, trans. and ed. Judith L. Kovacs (Grand Rapids: Eerdmans, 2005), vii.

[13] Matthew R. Malcolm, review of Yung Suk Kim, ed., *1 and 2 Corinthians*, Texts@Contexts ser., reviewed November 16, 2013, 3, 4, available on the website Review of Biblical Literature, https://www.bookreviews.org/bookdetail.asp?TitleId=9155.

[14] M. W. Dube Shomanah, "Postcolonial Biblical Interpretations," in *Methods of Biblical Interpretation*, 361.

While there is value in these approaches, there is also the danger that in the name of anti-imperial or anti-colonial readings of Scripture, a new imperialism is being enforced, in which the supposed "traditional" reader is silenced.

Liberation approaches specifically see liberation of the disempowered as a hermeneutical key to the Bible. If this opens up otherwise neglected elements of a text, it can be helpful. But in the book review mentioned earlier, I comment on one of the hazards of such an approach:

> I wonder whether the "liberation" agenda consciously set by this contextualized reading sometimes skews the context of the letter's first recipients. For example, the "weak" of 1 Cor 8 are read as the economically weak who had "little or no access to 'meat offered to idols'" (60). This reading is at odds with most readings of the chapter . . . , given that it seems that the "weak" of 1 Cor 8 are precisely those who are in danger of being lured to eat meat offered to idols.[15]

Feminist and *womanist* approaches aim to give special attention to female voices *in* the text, female readers *of* the text, and readings that problematize patriarchal assumptions or practices. *Queer* approaches destabilize readings of the Bible that assume or support traditional notions of gender or sexuality, seeking fresh ways of hearing the text and prioritizing the questions and interests of homosexual readers. In an article entitled "What Queer Hermeneutics Can Do for Us in Spain," for example, New Testament professor Luis Menéndez-Antuña argues that the binary conception of sexuality that traditional ("straight" or "gay") readers frequently bring to the Bible needs to be seen as a construct that colors one's reading of the relevant biblical texts.[16]

There is growing interest in geographical and ethnic readings of the Bible, seen in such fields as African hermeneutics, Latina/o hermeneutics, and Asian-American hermeneutics. An emerging area in the study of the New Testament is the foregrounding of *Jewish* sensibilities in considering the New Testament. Two key figures are Amy-Jill Levine, in relation to the Gospels, and Mark Nanos, in relation to the letters of Paul. Levine and Nanos are highly suspicious of readings that involve unnuanced and derogatory views of first-century Judaism, and they see Jesus and Paul as essentially Jewish teachers who operated within the parameters of first-century Judaism.

---

[15] Matthew R. Malcolm, review, p. 3.

[16] Luis Menéndez-Antuña, "What Queer Hermeneutics Can Do for Us in Spain," in Yung Suk Kim, ed., *1 and 2 Corinthians*, Texts@Contexts series (Minneapolis: Fortress Press, 2013), 158.

At the same time, as we saw in chapter 4, there is a great deal of present interest in unashamedly *Christian* or *theological* readings of Scripture, especially reading in sympathy with the early creeds and patristic interests. British theologian Tom Greggs wrote, "I . . . advocate that the activity of reading Scripture through the creeds and symbols of the first four councils is an exercise in reading Scripture with relational responsibility not only to the church of our own day, but to the communion of saints through all ages."[17]

Resources with Which to Question the Text

A key question in approaching the text is, which text? The field of *textual criticism* helps answer this question by examining the history of textual (manuscript) traditions.

Another key question is, what is the text? The fields of *genre criticism* and *canonical criticism* aim to contribute to this question. Genre criticism has developed with the aim of being attentive to formal discourse patterns that would have been recognizable to biblical writers and hearers. James L. Bailey, a professor of New Testament, defines genre as follows: "*Genres are the conventional and repeatable patterns of oral and written speech that facilitate interaction among people in specific social situations.* Decisive to this basic definition are three aspects: *patternedness, social setting,* and *rhetorical impact.*"[18]

Personally, I am cautious with regard to analysis of formal patterns of genre or rhetoric in the New Testament. In part, this is because the situation in which the New Testament documents arose was one of immense destabilizing of expectations, social settings, and cultural schemas. It may be that the very revolutionary nature of the Christ event opened up creative new literary production—particularly driven by the shape of the apostolic gospel(s). Nevertheless, considerations of genre are certainly of some value: the New Testament writers did not start from scratch. In his famous work on the canonical Gospels, for example, Professor Richard Burridge, a priest in the Church of England, finds *both* continuity (so, the genre *bioi,*) and discontinuity (so, the subgenre *bioi Iesou*).

Another question for the exegete is, what is the text about, as a whole? Numerous interpretive approaches have arisen to attempt to answer this question. *Rhetorical criticism* seeks to understand ancient ways of organizing persuasive speech. *Epistolary criticism* aims to understand conventions of ancient letters. *Discourse*

---

[17] Tom Greggs, "Biblical Hermeneutics and *Relational* Responsibility," in Porter and Malcolm, *The Future of Biblical Interpretation*, 94 (see chap. 4, n. 18).
[18] James L. Bailey, "Genre Analysis," in Green, *Hearing the New Testament*, 143.

analysis seeks to be attentive to large-scale syntactic connections. I will offer some considerations of rhetorical criticism in the example of my own research below.

Another key question is, how does the text communicate its points? Here various linguistic and literary resources are relevant, such as the fields of *narrative criticism* and *information structure*.

Diagramming is a means of visually depicting the syntactic relationships in a passage. It involves teasing apart paragraphs, sentences, and clauses so that their logic becomes more evident. For example, we might diagram 1 Pet 1:3–9—which is an extremely long and complex sentence—as follows (using my own somewhat wooden translation):

> Blessed is our God and Father of Jesus Christ,
> > Who has rebirthed us according to his great mercy,
> > > Into a living hope
> > > > Through the resurrection of Jesus Christ from the dead
> > > Into an inheritance that is undying and unblemished and unfading
> > > > Being kept in heaven for you
> > > > > Who by the power of God are guarded through faith for a salvation prepared to be revealed at the last time
> > > > > > In which you are rejoicing for a little while now, even if it is necessary for you to be grieved by various trials
> > > > > > > So that the testing of your faith . . .
> > > > > > > > Which is more valuable than gold
> > > > > > > > > Which is destructible, even though tested by fire
> > > > > > > > . . . Might be found to result in praise and glory and honor at the revelation of Jesus Christ
> > > > > > > > > Whom you love without having seen
> > > > > > > > > In whom you believe without seeing
> > > > > > > You rejoice with an unspeakable and glorious joy, receiving the goal of your faith: the salvation of your souls.

This example is a very basic form of diagramming, in which independent and dependent clauses are separated and lined up. The idea of this process is that it helps the exegete to recognize the main points, the sub-points, and how they relate.

Developing an Orientation of Expectant Curiosity

It would seem wise to adopt a range of reading strategies, which might be suggested occasion by occasion, as we "interview" a particular text. Our refining sensitivity to the biblical texts may direct us to one or the other strategy in a particular reading context. I tell my students that a key to good exegesis is *primed curiosity*—a stance, rather than a method.

We might say, then, that methods are both a help and a hindrance. They can be a hindrance when they box us in to an unnecessarily narrow—or even distorted—way of hearing the text. But they are a great help when they allow us to question and hear the text from particular vantage points.

BIG IDEA

Exegetical methods can be helpful in allowing us to give critical attention to various elements of the text. However, not all methods will be relevant for all texts. The nature of the text or the reading occasion may suggest the most fruitful methods to adopt in a particular instance. Some methods are useful for illuminating the location of the author/text; some are useful for illuminating the location of the reader(s); and some are useful in questioning the text itself.

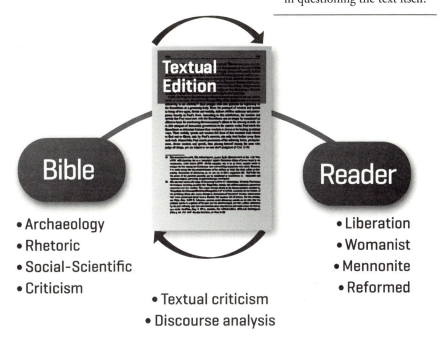

- Bible
  - Archaeology
  - Rhetoric
  - Social-Scientific
  - Criticism

- Textual Edition
  - Textual criticism
  - Discourse analysis

- Reader
  - Liberation
  - Womanist
  - Mennonite
  - Reformed

Figure 6.

Questions for Discussion

Examine some items of *biblical interpretation*. These might include a commentary, a devotional, or even your own exegesis paper!

1. What hermeneutical assumptions are betrayed by each example of biblical interpretation? For example, do any of the following statements resonate with the hermeneutical impulses of the biblical interpretation?

   - "I have direct, unmediated access to the biblical texts."
   - "My culture does not impact the way I read."
   - "Truth requires interpretive closure."
   - "Interpretive closure is always irresponsible."
   - "There is only one possible meaning."
   - "We can never know the meaning."
   - "The goal is to understand what was in the author's mind."
   - "The author's intentions are irrelevant."
   - "It is appropriate to go beyond the intentions of the author, so long as our interpretation is guided by the gospel."

2. What interpretive strategies are employed? For example . . .

   - consideration of the oral or literary sources behind the text
   - analysis of the historical backgrounds of the text
   - attention to the reception of the passage across history
   - consideration of questions raised by a feminist perspective
   - analysis of Greek word order
   - use of diagramming

3. How would you evaluate the use of these strategies? Could the item have benefited from other approaches?

For Further Reading

On the location of the author/text: see the resources mentioned in this chapter, as well as commentaries, which generally emphasize this dimension.

On the location of the reader: see the resources mentioned in this chapter and in chapter 3.

On analysis of the text itself:

Campbell, Constantine R. 2015. *Advances in the Study of Greek: New Insights for Reading the New Testament.* Grand Rapids: Zondervan.

In my PhD dissertation, I did not establish any singular "methodology" up front, and in fact never included a section on method. I should point out that my dissertation related to the interpretation of a text (1 Corinthians), rather than a topic in the hard or social sciences—for which sections on method are more important.

My research question related to the big picture of 1 Corinthians. I used to sum up my question in conversation with friends as: why does Paul cover those topics, in that order? In particular, I was intrigued as to why Paul deferred the crucial topic of the resurrection of the dead until the end of the letter. I had a hunch that this question might be illuminated by discourse analysis, epistolary criticism, *or* rhetorical criticism, *but I was also open to the possibility that* sociocultural *factors might have been influential, such as the influence of nearby Eleusis, a center of "mystery" religion. I visited* archaeological *sites at Corinth, Eleusis, Athens, and other locations, and considered whether an understanding of the* geography *and* history *behind the text might be helpful. At the same time, I wondered how others across* reception history *had thought about this question, and spent a good deal of time investigating the homilies of John Chrysostom. I even coordinated a study day on Chrysostom to hear from the experts! While all of this was going on, I labored repeatedly through the Greek text of 1 Corinthians and participated in a reading group that did the same.*

My frustration with rhetorical criticism *as a methodology was that it seemed, in most instances, to operate from the assumption that those who wrote in Greek utilized standard Greco-Roman organizing structures. Something about this did not sit right with me: I knew that Paul defined himself as a "Hebrew . . . of Hebrews" and an apostle of Jesus Christ (Phil 3:5; 1 Cor 1:1); and I wondered whether these factors might influence his rhetoric. It was in conversation with my father, a linguist, that I realized yet another interpretive field might bear fruit:* cognitive linguistics.

My father's own work had been to study the ways Australian aboriginal users of English draw upon mental imagery influenced by aboriginal culture when they communicate in English, even if they no longer speak aboriginal languages. It struck me that there was a parallel here to the situation of Paul, who was writing in Greek but was self-consciously a "Hebrew" and an "apostle." I looked further into cognitive and cultural linguistics *and found support for the idea that language—even at the level of discourse structure—is shaped by cultural imagery. It seemed to me that Paul's gospel of a crucified and risen Messiah drew on, and transformed, Jewish imagery of reversal, such that it became a key structure of Paul's thought. This motif was utilized by Paul (along with more "regular" features of Greek communication) in his letters, giving overall structure to 1 Corinthians itself. This seemed to me to help explain why the main body of 1 Corinthians begins with a devastating critique of Corinthian triumphalism with the cross (chapters 1–4), and ends with a devastating critique of Corinthian triumphalism with the resurrection (chapter 15).*

There was more to my dissertation than this, of course, but the point here is that there was not a singular method that allowed this exegetical destination. What was constant, however, was inquisitive curiosity and a conviction that the text might surprise me.

Metzger, Bruce M., ed. 1994. *A Textual Commentary on the Greek New Testament.* Second edition. New York: United Bible Societies.

Porter, Stanley E. 2015. *Linguistic Analysis of the Greek New Testament: Studies in Tools, Methods, and Practice.* Grand Rapids: Baker Academic.

Tov, Emanuel. 2011. *Textual Criticism of the Hebrew Bible.* Third edition. Minneapolis: Augsburg Fortress.

10

INTERPRETING THE OLD TESTAMENT

In this chapter we will follow the logic developed so far in considering "Christian interpretation" as arising from general hermeneutics. Thus, we will first consider *priming for the Old Testament*, and then consider *the Old Testament as Christian Scripture*. Finally, we will apply this to the exegesis of the famous story of David and Goliath in 1 Samuel 17.

Priming for the Old Testament

Realm

Two provisional realms to consider for works of the Old Testament are the Hebrew canon on the one hand, and the Christian canon(s) on the other.[1] The Christian Bible is different both because it includes two parts, of which this one is considered "old" or "first"; and because it follows the arrangement of the Septuagint. While the Hebrew Bible is arranged according to *law*, *prophets*, and *writings* (see Luke 24:44), the Christian Old Testament is arranged according to *law*, *history*, *wisdom*, and *prophets*.

Taking the example of 1–2 Samuel (which we will go on using throughout this chapter), in the Christian Bible they are two works, fitting neatly into the *history* section of the Old Testament. In the Hebrew Bible they are one work, fitting into the *Prophets*. Neither "realm" needs to be given immediate priority, but

---

[1] Of course, one could also think of other "realms," such as early Hebrew/Israelite/Jewish literature.

the nature of each is worth exploring: if we characterize Samuel from the outset as "history," what will that mean for the way it is heard? If we characterize it as "prophecy," what will this entail? (This also brings the further question: what did prophecy mean at the time of the formation of the Hebrew canon?)

Mission

To what overarching mission do the works of the Hebrew Bible/Old Testament contribute? Many answers could be given to this question, depending on the specific biblical book:

- telling divine history
- pursuing civic unity
- pursuing national holiness
- justifying Israel's actions
- justifying God in the face of Israel's defeats

Continuing with the example of the book(s) of Samuel, one needs to consider *why* this story is told. Is this explained, for example, by Martin Noth's idea of a "Deuteronomistic history"?[2]

Although the name makes it sound as though it refers to the background of Deuteronomy, actually the "Deuteronomistic history" refers to the books of the Hebrew Bible that explain Israel's history from wilderness to exile, in the light of the Deuteronomic covenant. Specifically, this includes the books of Deuteronomy, Joshua, Judges, Samuel, and Kings. These books are said to have received their final redaction (edition) at the time of the exile, an editorial process that sought to situate the exile as a covenantal curse.

Certainly, in its canonical form and location, Samuel is part of a broader literary expanse that stretches from the Deuteronomic covenant to the covenantal curse of exile. Within this expanse, the book of Samuel displays the rise of kingship. But is this Deuteronomistic historical perspective a *sufficient* account of the "mission" of the work? A number of scholars express reservations. There does seem to be a degree of ambivalence in Samuel regarding the promise or threat posed by kingship, David, obedience, and cult. Is it even possible or useful to identify a singular "mission" from which such a complex work springs?

I do think it is possible and useful, so long as we are not overambitious! My proposal is that, without necessarily having a singular apologetic function in mind (such as the justification of God's dealings with Israel in the light of the

---

[2] See Martin Noth, *The Deuteronomistic History*, 2nd ed. (n.p.: Sheffield Academic Press, 2002).

Babylonian defeat), the book of Samuel seeks to attest *God's acts in history*. This mission depends on the conviction that God's acts are purposeful and able to be grasped to a degree—but it allows a certain openness to the exact destination and interpretation of these purposeful acts.

In other words, like other historical narrative in the Old Testament/Hebrew Bible, the books of Samuel tell *prophetic history, with an eschatological orientation*.

Emergence

Four elements of the emergence of Old Testament texts that are worthy of consideration are *geography, history, society,* and *literary conventions*.

Geography

The Old Testament narratives focus on the land of ancient Israel, its neighbor Egypt to the southwest, and its neighbors Assyria and Babylon to the northeast (as well as other nations in between, such as Moab). For many parts of the Old Testament, it is essential to have a basic understanding of this geography in order to make sense of characters' movements and prophetic declarations.

For example, in the books of Samuel, it is helpful to understand the many locations that are referenced. Many of the battle scenes are hard to understand without a map. A map of the region of the valley of Elah greatly illuminates the face-off between the Israelites and the Philistines that led to the encounter between David and Goliath.

History

Unlike the New Testament, the Old Testament covers a massive stretch of time. So, for different parts of the Old Testament, different historical backgrounds are relevant. Complicating things further, issues of historicity are much more difficult for the Old Testament period than the New, in part due to the greater number and complexity of documents, and in part due to the relative lack of archaeological illumination.

Debates about the historicity of Old Testament texts became very heated in the twentieth century, with some arguing for the straightforward reliability of the Old Testament narratives, and others arguing that these narratives preserved traditions that had been significantly redacted for political purposes in the time of the exile.

We saw earlier that Martin Noth is particularly known for his development of the idea of a "Deuteronomistic history," that is, the proposal that the books from Deuteronomy to Kings were redacted at the time of the exile, with the redactor bringing numerous elements into line with the Deuteronomic idea that Israel's history would be governed by covenant blessing and curse.

The possibility of exilic redaction need not necessarily go along with doubts about the historicity of the traditions preserved in the biblical material. It needs to be recognized that there are "maximalists" and "minimalists" in scholarship concerning Israel's early history, as well as a spectrum in between.

What this means for our ongoing example of the books of Samuel is that they must be considered not only in terms of the history they report, but also—*if* an exilic final edition is accurate—in terms of the later historical situation to which the final form of the work was directed: what was the narrator/editor hoping to achieve with this text?

Society

It is impossible to make a general summary about the society of Israel over the course of the Old Testament's narratives. Nevertheless, by the end of the Old Testament period (i.e., the postexilic period), numerous features had emerged. These should be thought of as mainstream, without denying the possibility of exceptions. In terms of *beliefs*, these mainstream features must include: *monotheism, election of Israel, land as possessed inheritance (of which the temple was symbolically central), Torah as God's guiding Word to his people*, and *eschatological hope as the orientation of Israel's corporate life*. In terms of *behaviors*, mainstream features would include: *the keeping of Sabbath, festivals, food laws*, and *circumcision*.[3]

That "temple" was such an important institution should be kept in mind, for example, in seeing that the book of Samuel ends with David installing a place of sacrifice in Jerusalem. Although the book itself doesn't draw out the full significance of this event, it should not be neglected by the interpreter, as it suggests something very important about David's legacy.

Literary conventions

There are numerous genres that appear in the Old Testament. We will consider key exegetical questions to ask when we encounter *narrative, law*, and *poetry*.

Whereas stories today might be told in 280-character chunks, with pictures and video clips thrown in, *Hebrew narrative* carries the expectation of being read publicly in large stretches. It frequently evidences careful planning of plot development, and it seeks culturally informed hearers equipped with patience, an ear

---

[3] I am grateful to Allan Chapple at Trinity Theological College (Perth), who uses categories similar to these in capturing the key features of Second Temple Judaism.

for subtlety, and an investment in the characters. A number of specific questions may be useful for the interpreter of narrative in the Hebrew Bible/Old Testament:

1. How does the passage fit into a larger plot development?

2. Are there devices (such as repeated plot markers or locational shifts or *inclusio*) that indicate the parameters of a particular section?

3. How might the passage be divided into "scenes"?

4. Why was each event selected for inclusion? What does it add to the story being told? Are certain events given more space than others? Why? Are certain events left out? Why?

5. Are any details labored over redundantly? Why might this be the case?

6. Is there symbolic weight invested in a particular character/event/detail?

7. What cultural conceptualizations are assumed in the text?

8. Is the narrator siding with a particular character?

9. What does the passage leave ambiguous? What does it ensure is unambiguous?

My conviction is that *Hebrew law* rests—either explicitly or implicitly—on the foundation of covenant. That is, because the Lord, as King, had saved Israel for himself, they were brought into a formal relationship that involved certain obligations. This model (and particularly the book of Deuteronomy) has frequently been compared to the treaty systems of the ancient Near East (though with numerous differences). Comparison with ancient Near Eastern legal systems can be fruitful for the interpreter. Numerous questions are generally worth asking when considering legal material in the Bible:

1. Is this law explicitly or implicitly part of a covenantal context? How should this impact its interpretation?

2. Does this law come in the context of a series of laws that aim to maintain faithfulness to God? Does it come in a series that aims to maintain holiness or purity of the nation? How do the laws around it situate it?

3. Would this law have had the effect of altering or forbidding an existing practice?

4. How do these laws compare/contrast with others from the ancient Near East?

5. How would this law have been enacted in the land? How might its enactment have been made more complex by the division of the kingdom or the loss of the temple?

6. How was this law interpreted by those who considered themselves to be under it?

7. Are there elements of ancient Israelite culture that illuminate these laws?

Hebrew poetry is somewhat different from the poetry that modern English-language hearers might be used to, whether they are more familiar with the poetry of Dr. Seuss or Michael Symmons Roberts. The late pastor and professor Rick Byargeon suggested, "When there is a higher degree of density and structure, the text is more poetic, but when there is less terseness and structure, the text is more prosaic."[4] One of the features of Hebrew poetry is parallelism, in which a line is reiterated, or countered, or extended, by a subsequent, parallel line. Another feature is concentration of imagery. A number of specific questions present themselves as useful:

1. What is the mood of the passage?

2. What impression is created by the use of imagery?

3. What sort of parallelism is used? What effect does it produce?

4. Are there features of general "wisdom" that are evidenced here? How do they differ from law or narrative?

Reception

Any substantial consideration of the reception of Old Testament texts must do justice to at least two important trajectories of impact: *Judaism* and *Christianity*. The impacts in these areas are not only seen in written interpretation (though that is important), but also in cultural schemas, festivals, liturgies, songs, and other elements. We have seen already that the Jewish festival of Purim is importantly related to the book of Esther. The post-history of the Song of Moses in Exodus would include other songs, such as those by Hannah, David, Judith, Mary, and the saints in Revelation.

---

[4] Rick Byargeon, "Listening to the Lyrics," in Bruce Corley, Steve W. Lemke, and Grant L. Lovejoy, *Biblical Hermeneutics: A Comprehensive Introduction to Interpreting Scripture*, 2nd ed. (Nashville: B&H, 2002), 280.

Going back to our example of the books of Samuel, it is also important to consider echoes and recapitulations in the rest of the Old Testament itself (though I recognize that this raises questions about relative dating). For example, God's covenant with David in 2 Samuel 7 has an important reception history within the rest of the Old Testament:[5] In Psalm 2, the "sonship" of the Davidic king is affirmed; in Psalm 78, the selection of David (as shepherd-king) is recalled; Psalm 89 carries an extended reflection on the Davidic covenant; in Isaiah 7–11, the covenant is presupposed; Isaiah 55 uses the language of covenant to describe God's promises to David and the people; Jeremiah 33 expresses hope for the future on the basis of God's promises to David; in Hosea 3 there is an assumption that a Davidic king must one day arise; in Amos 9, the commitment to the Davidic line is presumed; in Zechariah 6, the covenant with David provides a basis for future hope.

Given that this is the key way the book of Samuel is recalled in the rest of Scripture, it would seem that this book was *received* as being chiefly about God's covenant promises to his anointed king. With reception history as our guide, then, we might approach this book with the provisional expectation that it will tell the story of God's covenant with David. This might then raise further questions for us as we read it: why is so much time spent on Samuel and Saul? Why begin what was perceived to be the story of David with the story of Hannah? Does the New Testament use the book of Samuel with the same focus?

The Old Testament as Christian Scripture

The Christian interpreter, of course, is interested in all of the preceding features and can converse with any other reader with the assumption that such features might be agreed to be significant. But as we have seen, Christian interpretation brings some special areas of interest.

Theology, Canon, Gospel

We have seen already that the Christian interpreter will bring to the Scriptures the refined (but provisional) insights of systematic theology, which can guide his reading. In different Christian settings, theological systems will have certain differences. But across the board, the theological pre-understanding that the Christian interpreter brings to the Bible finds the boundaries of its polyphony in the canon

---

[5] See William M. Schniedewind, *Society and the Promise to David: The Reception History of 2 Samuel 7:1–17* (Oxford: Oxford University Press, 1999)—a work from which I draw here—for a reception history of 2 Samuel 7. I follow Schniedewind's choice of scriptural passages.

and the center of its coherence in the gospel of Jesus Christ. It will be fruitful to spend some time considering how these elements will impact Christian interpretation of the Old Testament.

For the Christian interpreter, the Bible as a whole points ultimately to Jesus Christ. Thus, a canon-aware "Christian interpretation" of any particular book will necessarily be different in some regards from a Jewish interpretation of the same book, because the canonical context is broader. For the Christian, each Old Testament voice is one of the "different ways" that God spoke to his people before his climactic speech in his Son (Heb 1:1). It is these same words that are said, in general, to testify to Jesus (Luke 24) and his gospel (Romans 3; 1 Corinthians 15). Each Old Testament book might therefore be seen to build on what comes before in the canon, and look ahead to the fulfilment to come.

It is essential, then, for the Christian interpreter to ask how any Old Testament passage under consideration relates to the gospel of Jesus Christ. But Christian conceptions of the relationship of Christ to the Old Testament vary. For Augustine, the Old Testament depicted *precept* and *promise*; for Luther, it similarly presented *law* and *gospel*. For Calvin, it prepared for Christ and prefigured him typologically. We must come to consider how it is that the gospel of Jesus Christ should actually impact Christian interpretation of the Old Testament.

Does the gospel come as the fitting answer to the problems and expectations raised by the Old Testament or does the gospel summon Christian readers to adjust their reading of the Old Testament to fit its newfound conclusion? There is some debate about this. For example, Walter Kaiser argues that the New Testament writers use the Old Testament in a way that fits exactly with the singular intentions of the Old Testament authors, who anticipated the events of the first century. Thus, there is a forward movement from Old Testament to New.[6] Richard Hays, on the other hand, argues that it is necessary to "read backwards" from Jesus to the Old Testament. He stated that "it would be a hermeneutical blunder to read the Law and the Prophets as deliberately *predicting* events in the life of Jesus."[7]

My own position is that we do not need to choose between reading forwards or reading backwards, but that both are parts of responsible Christian interpretation. That is, we should acknowledge *both* that the Law and the Prophets are

---

[6] See Walter C. Kaiser, *The Uses of the Old Testament in the New* (Eugene, OR: Wipf and Stock, 1985); Kenneth Berding and Jonathan Lunde, eds., *Three Views on the New Testament Use of the Old Testament* (Grand Rapids: Zondervan, 2008).

[7] Hays, *Reading Backwards*, 93–94 (see chap. 7, n. 21).

pregnant with weight beyond their initial circumstances, *and* that the event of Jesus's coming triggers a dramatic new perspective on the Old Testament Scriptures, which had not previously been demanded.

For example, the books of Samuel and Kings do not attempt to neatly tie up the strands of David's character, or see God's promises to him as exhausted in Solomon, but leave room for the expectation of a future son/anointed. The text itself has an eschatological lean to it. The text is pregnant with expectation. (And, of course, different Old Testament texts are pregnant to very different degrees.)

But on the other hand, the Law and the Prophets give birth to a surprising Messiah, in the light of whose coming the Law and Prophets themselves must be creatively quizzed and reread. As the author of the Epistle to the Hebrews recognizes, even certain silences of the Old Testament suddenly take on a bigger significance than they could possibly have had before (Heb 7:3). Like the ending of an Agatha Christie novel, the gospel provides a conclusion that is both entirely fitting and remarkably surprising, such that one can excitedly revisit the earlier chapters and find new significance that had not previously been evident. In other words, a messianic reading of the Old and New Testaments is *both* prospective and retrospective.

I have reflected on the significance of this for the Christian interpreter elsewhere:

> Therefore, in considering the New Testament appropriation of Scriptural resources, there are three complex stages to consider: first, the varied *initial readings* of the Scriptures before Christ; second, the *crisis* of the Christ event itself, including the actions and teachings of his life, as well as the claims and experiences of his death, resurrection, and ascension as Spirit-sending Lord; third, the *renegotiation* of Scripture in the light of this culture-shifting crisis.[8]

I remember when I saw the movie The Sixth Sense *and (spoiler alert) I reached the climactic scene in which it was revealed that the main character had been dead all along. I had missed this altogether, but suddenly began to realize that certain details in the earlier moments of the film had been far more important than I had assumed—including the silences! It seems to me that this must have been the experience of the disciples on the road to Emmaus, when Jesus opened their eyes to understand all that the Scriptures had said about him (see* Luke 24:13–35*). Their realization was* retrospective, *in the light of Jesus. But they could now see that the Old Testament itself had been looking forward* to this moment, *in ways that had previously been shrouded in mystery.*

---

[8] Matthew R. Malcolm, "God Has Spoken: The Renegotiation of Scripture in Hebrews," in Malcolm, *All That the Prophets Have Declared*, 173 (see chap. 7, n. 17).

It is possible for Christian interpreters to follow these same steps in considering the relationship between a particular Old Testament passage and the gospel of Jesus Christ: they can consider the *initial readings* before Christ; they can consider the many facets of the *crisis* of the Christ event; and they can consider ways that the passage might be *renegotiated* with new significance in the light of this crisis event. This new significance might be, for example, that the general eschatological lean of the passage toward a new shepherd-king can now be seen as a promise of Christ himself.

An Example: David and Goliath

In this famous story (1 Samuel 17) Goliath is repeatedly referred to as "the Philistine." Perhaps this feature of the story marks it as open to typological reading:[9] After this feature is repeated numerous times, the hearer senses that we are encountering "types" or "categories" here; not just individuals: "the Philistine" and "the shepherd." This is further heightened as we find that the narrator shows both opponents making appeal to their *gods* at the near-climactic moment: this is, in fact, not just a battle between the shepherd and the Philistine, but between the Lord and the Philistine gods.

It seems, then, that this Former Prophet narrative opens itself to typological significance. Such a reading of the text is not just foisted on a completely unsuspecting text by later precritical Christian interests. Francis Watson, a professor of New Testament exegesis, makes a good point: "What is proposed is not an anachronistic return to pre-critical exegesis but a radicalization of the modern theological and exegetical concern to identify ever more precisely those characteristics that are peculiar to the biblical texts."[10]

I am suggesting that "typological pregnancy" is indeed a characteristic of biblical texts. Goliath, in Scripture, was never *just* Goliath. He was symbolic of a category—a category that might grow and evolve as the story attested by the Scriptures progresses.

Chrysostom is not to be scoffed at, then, as he reached a peculiarly Christian reading of the chapter, with the stone in the shepherd's bag typifying Christ himself: "Therefore, let us take in our hands that stone, I mean the cornerstone, the spiritual rock. If Paul could think in these terms of the rock in the desert, no one

---

[9] I am not entirely happy with the terminology of "typology," but will use it (sparingly) until I find something better.

[10] Cited in James M. Hamilton Jr., "The Typology of David's Rise to Power: Messianic Patterns in the Book of Samuel," *SBJT* 16, no. 2 (2012): 4.

will in any way feel resentment against me if I understand David's stone in the same sense."[11]

The stone was always pregnant with possibility; and Chrysostom was here suggesting that Christian readers can perceive it to have been pregnant with Christ. This is evocative of Bede's consideration of the Old Testament as both water and wine. It is water for any who will take it as such; but it transcends water for the Christian interpreter, and becomes wine.

Christian Interpretation and Ministry Application

I imagine that this still appears somewhat "subjective" and does not offer firm constraints on *when* it is appropriate to draw Christological connections. But it should be recalled that the hermeneutical enterprise is bigger than just the discernment of the author's intentions. This means that our interpretive comments need not always be phrased as though they are recovering such intentions. It could be possible, in speaking of the stone of David as Christ in a ministry setting, to phrase oneself in a way that quite openly draws attention to the Christian location of the reader: "The *Christian* reader cannot help but recall the burden of the New Testament that Christ himself is God's surprising, conquering stone." Or: "This reminds *me* of 1 Peter, where Jesus is the stone . . ."

Like the reader of the haiku poem, these sorts of statements are openly saying, "This is where the passage takes *me*," without claiming that this resonance was already in the mind of the human author. Notice that Chrysostom did in fact draw attention to himself in his discussion of David's stone.

As another example, consider Charles Spurgeon's sermon on Ezekiel's deserted infant:

> Doubtless the Lord here describes the Jewish people when they began to multiply in the land of Egypt, and were grievously oppressed by Pharaoh. Pharaoh had commanded them to cast out the male children that they might perish. Hence, the figure of an infant deserted, cast out into the open field to perish by wild beasts, by starvation, or exposure, was a very apt portrait of the youthful state of Israel, when God looked upon her in love, and brought her out of Egypt to set her in a goodly land. But all the best divines and expositors concur in the belief that we have here also a most extraordinarily apt, and significant description of the human race by nature, and of the way in which God in divine mercy passes by

---

[11] Cited in John R. Franke, ed., *Joshua, Judges, Ruth, 1–2 Samuel*, Ancient Christian Commentary on Scripture (Downers Grove, IL: IVP Academic, 2005), 274.

the sinner when utterly lost and helpless, and by the power of the Spirit, bids him "Live." At any rate, we intend to consider it so this morning.[12]

Notice that, just as Chrysostom drew attention to his own place as a reader, and just as Bede drew attention to the potential for the Old Testament to be read as water and as wine, Spurgeon acknowledged both the impact of the history of lived readings of the text, and the possibility of two levels of reading. He recognized that in its first hearing, his text was about the infancy of Israel in Egypt, but he considered that the weight of Christian reception of the passage afforded him space to detect a further level of significance for the Christian interpreter in the age of the Spirit of Jesus Christ: it is by "the power of the Spirit" (sent by Christ) that God enables those who were dead to live.

Although one might debate the particular applications by Chrysostom, Bede, or Spurgeon, their hermeneutical impulse flows from the trajectory set by Jesus himself in Luke 24: all Scripture finds its fulfilment in the person and work of Jesus.

An Exegetical Case Study: 1 Samuel 17

Let us apply all that we have seen to the exegesis of 1 Samuel 17, the famous chapter about David and Goliath. Rather than producing a finished exegesis paper, I aim here to take you into the process of exegesis itself, showing the sorts of "primed questions" that I would raise at each point. In the next chapter, when we focus on New Testament exegesis, I will instead provide a completed exegesis paper on a particular passage. You will notice below that I am assuming that I have already been "primed" for exegesis of 1 Samuel, but I have not yet looked at the secondary literature relating to the particular passage under consideration. I think this is a useful practice: to approach the text with an acknowledgment of my indebtedness to former readings, but deferring the use of commentaries until I have conducted my own analysis of the text.

Approaching the Text

Having already primed myself for the exegesis of 1 Samuel, I have already developed a map of its contents. As I approach the specific passage of 1 Samuel 17, I remind myself of this overview:

---

[12] C. H. Spurgeon, "Ezekiel's Deserted Infant: No. 468," a sermon delivered on September 7, 1868, available as spurgeongems.org, accessed July 28, 2017, http://www.spurgeongems.org/vols7-9/chs468.pdf.

1 Sam 1–6	Hannah, Samuel, ark	Hannah's song of praise
1 Sam 7–12	Saul appointed king	
1 Sam 13–15	Saul rejected as king	
1 Sam 16–31	**David anointed and persecuted**	
2 Sam 1–4	Saul dies and David ascends	David's song of lament
2 Sam 5–7	David receives kingship and oath	
2 Sam 8–12	David fights and sins	
2 Sam 13–19	Strife among David's sons	
2 Sam 20–24	David is faithful and sinful	David's song of deliverance

This passage comes toward the beginning of the long stretch in which David is depicted as the anointed but persecuted future king. We might therefore expect this event to build on chapter 16 in establishing this reputation.

I now read through the whole of chapter 17 in English, considering its aesthetic impact, thinking about the initial questions that it raises, and attempting to hear its big idea. The reason for reading it in English initially is so that the overall rhythm of the whole passage might not be lost in the painstaking rigor of translating Hebrew. At this point, I might come up with something like: "God's anointed future king defeats his enemies." My hope is that this provisional sense will be refined by the time I am through the exegetical process.

I attempt to discern the flow of the passage as follows. Because it is narrative, I divide it into scenes:

- 1–11: Scene 1: The Philistine champion in the Valley of Elah
- 12–18: Scene 2: David in Bethlehem
- 19–30: Scene 3: David goes to the battle
- 31–37: Scene 4: David meets Saul
- 38–51: Scene 5: David defeats Goliath
- 51–54: Scene 6: The routing of the Philistines
- 55–58: Scene 7: The king's inquiry

Observing the Text

At this point I come to engage in curious questioning of the (Hebrew) text, seeking to discern answers as best I can from the text itself.

Verses 1–11: scene 1: The Philistine champion in the Valley of Elah

Verses 1–3

Where are these locations? Can I make use of maps from Bible software? I note that the events at the major locations are interspersed in the narrative, with close-ups of the dialogue between David and other characters.

Verses 4–7

Who was the last tall man we encountered in the book of Samuel? It was Saul. Is there any significance here?

What is the big impact of this description? It seems to create dread. I note the textual discrepancy between Qumran/LXX and the Masoretic Text here in terms of Goliath's height.

Verses 8–10

What is the point of Goliath's question, "Am I not a Philistine, and are you not servants of Saul?" Is this really what defines the Israelites? Is the line "Are you not servants of Saul?" loaded with extra significance for those who have heard the story of Samuel so far?

I am reminded of Samuel's warnings about what kings would be like in chapter 8.

Why is the king of the Philistines/Gath not mentioned? Perhaps we are seeing the outcome of the people's desire to have a head-and-shoulders-taller, army-leading king, as the other nations have: this tall king (Saul) is actually outdone by the nations.

What is the impact of referring to Goliath as "the Philistine" in verse 10? I will hold on to this question as I continue to proceed.

Verse 11

I note again that Goliath is referred to not as "Goliath" or "the giant" or "the champion" or "the Gittite" but as "the Philistine." Perhaps this feature of the story marks it as open to typological significance: this is not just a battle between two individuals, but is symbolic of a struggle between Israel and her key enemy.

Verses 12–18: scene 2: David in Bethlehem

Verse 12

Why do we have this introduction, given that we have already seen Jesse and his sons in the previous chapter? I realize that there might be manuscript issues, but could there be rhetorical reasons for reintroducing these characters at this point? I will hold on to this thought.

Is there any significance in reiterating the location? Why is the narrator belaboring this?

Verses 13–15

How does verse 15 fit with 16:22? It is not inconceivable that they are both concurrently true.

Verse 16

I note yet again that Goliath is called "the Philistine." What is the point of this apparent aside?

Verses 17–18

Why are we told the specifics of the task? Why does the narrator choose to spend time on this? What are we supposed to notice?

Verses 19–30: scene 3: David goes to the battle

Verse 19

Does the reference to fighting mean that, concurrent with Goliath's summons, the nations are engaged in combat? Or does the "fighting" consist, at this moment, of waiting for the outcome of the champion's summons?

Verse 20

I note that regardless of the previous chapter's point that David moved from Jesse's service into Saul's service, the present chapter sees it as crucial that David was a shepherd (vv. 15, 20, 28, 34–35, 40). Could this be one reason for the reintroduction of David as son of Jesse in this chapter? And could this explain why the narrator has been belaboring certain elements?

I recall that pharaohs were presented as shepherds, having the shepherd's crook as a sign of their rule.

Verses 21–23

Are we to pick up any contrast with Saul, who hid among the baggage, and David, who left the baggage to go to the ranks?

Verses 24–27

I note that this part of the scene shows the Israelites speaking among themselves (24–25) before David arrives (26–27). I wonder, what is the effect of allowing us to eavesdrop on the Israelite soldiers' discussion before David enters? Perhaps it draws attention to the fact that David's question is slightly different from theirs: he is more disturbed that the Philistine is defying God.

What does it mean that the king will "make the house of his father free in Israel"? The *Brown-Driver-Briggs Hebrew Lexicon* suggests they would be "free from taxes, obligations, etc." Note the CSB: "will also make the family of that man's father exempt from paying taxes in Israel" (v. 25).

Verses 28–30

I note that this interaction with Eliab reminds the reader of several things: David is not the eldest among his brothers; David is a shepherd; and David provokes persecution simply by showing up the inaction of others. In this sense, Eliab seems to be reminiscent of Saul here, as once again the narrator draws attention to David's identity as a shepherd.

Verses 31–37: scene 4: David Meets Saul

Verses 31–33

I note that while there are a lot of questions about textual integrity in this chapter, these verses do not themselves imply that Saul is unfamiliar with David. (Consider that 16:21 had said that Saul loved David greatly.)

But how does verse 33 fit with 16:18? Is David a valiant warrior or a novice youth?

I note this so that I can later look into how the secondary literature deals with this problem.

Verses 34–37

I note that David explicitly links his ability to defeat "the Philistine" with his heritage as a shepherd (cf. 2 Sam 7; 24:17). This explanation by David is given a surprising amount of space in the story, which draws attention to this element as noteworthy. The one who is able to defeat the giant Philistine is not the "head-and-shoulders-above-the-rest" king of an army (which is what Israel had requested), but rather the shepherd, raised up by God.

The emphasis on the Lord's saving power is notable here; it is a theme of Samuel as a whole.

Verses 38–51: scene 5: David defeats Goliath

Verses 38–40

It seems to me that these verses could be removed without disturbing the flow. So, what does this section contribute to the narrative? I reread with this question in mind.

Is the traditional idea that David is *small* actually emphasized in the passage at all? I notice that what is emphasized is David's identity as a shepherd: he takes his shepherd staff and his shepherd's bag, rather than the king's armor.

Verses 41–44

Again, Goliath is referred to as "the Philistine." Once again, then, it seems that we are encountering "types" or "categories" here, not just individuals. This is further heightened as we find that the narrator shows both opponents making appeal to their *gods* at this tense moment: this is, in fact, not just a battle between David and the Philistine, but between the Lord and the Philistine gods.

The reference to the shield-bearer increases the almost comical contrast of the opponents.

I note the verbal link to 16:12, where David was first introduced as ruddy and handsome. Is there significance here?

Verses 45–47

Here, in case we missed the narrator's hints, David seems to spell out for us the two lessons that we are supposed to learn:

- The Lord is God (v. 46).
- The battle is the Lord's (v. 47).

Here truly is a man after God's own heart. I recall from my priming that both of these lessons are crucial in the book of Samuel more broadly:

- *The Lord of hosts* is the great reverser, who brings down and lifts up.
- *Israel* does not therefore need a head-and-shoulders-taller, army-leading king, as the nations have.

I note that although David's trust in the Lord is exemplary, it is not the special focus of the narrator here.

Verses 48–51

I am struck that at this climax of the narrative, reference is made (again) to David's shepherd's bag. Could it be that it is more important to the narrator that David is a shepherd than that David is small? I wonder, is this picked up elsewhere in the history of reception of this passage?

Verses 51b–54: scene 6: The routing of the Philistines

Verses 51–52

How does this action take place? Will this be illuminated by the use of maps? I look to my Bible software to see.

Verse 53

I notice the element of plunder: the Lord has won a victory and plunder without any help from the king who had promised riches (v. 25).

Verse 54

This is a striking intrusion to the text: Jerusalem has not yet been taken. This verse anticipates David's future. Why? Perhaps this alerts the reader that we are witnessing a key event in the history of David and Israel.

Verses 55–58: scene 7: The king's inquiry

It strikes me that this inquiry by "the king" is positioned comically late in the story. Neither the king nor his commander knows the identity of the one who defeated "the Philistine." David's answer reinforces again the link to his shepherding heritage.

I reason: the fact that we were shown David and Saul in discussion in verses 31–37 shows us that the narrator is fully aware that hearers will expect Saul to know David already. These verses are thus *supposed* to be surprising. Could it be that the chronological "problem" of Saul's knowing David in chapter 16 may in fact not be so problematic as it first appears: regardless of the extent to which Saul has had previous interaction with David, the narrator wants us to be struck by how blind Saul is to the man after God's own heart.

I make a note to look later into how the commentators deal with matters of chronological sequence.

Having worked through the passage, I now turn to the secondary literature, to see how commentators deal with the questions I have raised, as well as any questions I have missed.

Interacting with the Text

At this point, I seek to refine my previous, provisional sense of the big idea by considering what themes or emphases emerged that I hadn't fully recognized at the beginning. In particular, I would have to acknowledge that I had originally missed the significance of David's identity as *the shepherd*.

I consider how this chapter moves the narrative of the book forward. My sense, after working through the exegetical questioning in which I just engaged, is that it shows in microcosm what the whole book of Samuel seeks to display: that the Lord accomplishes victory and delights to use David, the trusting shepherd, rather than Saul, the stereotypical king-like-the-nations-have.

I consider how my reading of the passage has raised questions about the popular reception of this story—particularly the place of David as shepherd, rather than an emphasis on David's smallness. At this point I would revisit the history of reception of the passage.

I would also ask—given my Christian convictions about canon—how this passage prepares for the coming of Jesus: Is there more in this passage that

Christian readers might discern than was perceptible to pre-Christian hearers? To what degree is this passage "pregnant" with Jesus? I would note that David's defeat of Goliath is seen by many as symbolic of Christ's victory over the devil.

I am conscious that I have been reading this chapter as someone who has never endured a battle. I wonder how hearers in different circumstances to my own might read this chapter. This would lead me to look into reflections on the chapter by differently located interpreters.

Finally, I would ask: How should this passage impact God's people? In particular, I would consider how the Lord's ability to win victory should impact the way I and my fellow church members ought to think about our own situations in life, as well as society more broadly. Do these impacts attune me to hear anything further in the text that I might have missed previously?

BIG IDEA

Interpretation of the Old Testament involves giving attention to specific features of the Hebrew Bible's locatedness, as well as recognizing the Old Testament's special status as Christian Scripture. In particular, this will involve recognizing that it bears witness to Jesus Christ. Exegesis of the Old Testament (as of the New Testament) ought to involve primed inquisitiveness.

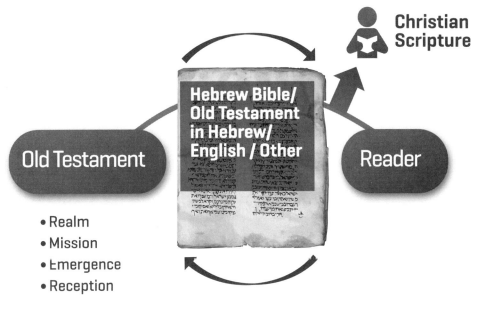

- Realm
- Mission
- Emergence
- Reception

Figure 7.

Questions for Discussion

1. What are some valid "realms" that a reader might posit for the Old Testament documents?

2. Is it possible to speak of a "mission" from which books of the Old Testament arise? Were they consciously produced as Scripture?

3. What are the most important features of the emergence of the Old Testament documents in the centuries before the Common Era?

4. What traditions of interpreting the Old Testament can you identify? How do they exert influence on present-day interpreters?

5. How would you evaluate the "live exegesis" of 1 Samuel in this chapter?

6. How can you develop an approach of primed curiosity when reading the Bible?

For Further Reading

Barton, John. 1996. *Reading the Old Testament: Method in Biblical Study.* Louisville: Westminster John Knox Press.

Briggs, Richard S. 2010. *The Virtuous Reader: Old Testament Narrative and Interpretive Virtue.* Grand Rapids: Baker Academic.

Moberly, Walter. 2013. *Old Testament Theology: Reading the Hebrew Bible as Christian Scripture.* Grand Rapids: Baker Academic.

Pratt, Richard L. 1990. *He Gave Us Stories: The Bible Student's Guide to Interpreting Old Testament Narratives.* Phillipsburg, NJ: P&R.

Stuart, Douglas. 2001. *Old Testament Exegesis: A Handbook for Students and Pastors.* Third edition. Louisville: Westminster John Knox Press.

11

INTERPRETING THE NEW TESTAMENT

I n this chapter, again, we will follow the logic developed so far in considering "Christian interpretation" as arising from general hermeneutics. Thus, we will first consider "priming" for the New Testament and then consider the New Testament as Christian Scripture. Finally, we will see how this might be applied to an exegesis paper on 1 Corinthians 13:1–3.

Priming for the New Testament

Realm

An important realm of New Testament documents for any reader would be that of early Christian literature. This immediately situates them as part of an emerging movement within Judaism, centered around Jesus as Messiah. The emphasis in today's scholarship is on diversity in such literature—which extends beyond canonical boundaries. It is certainly not inappropriate to bring New Testament documents into dialogue with a breadth of other early material, even if, for the Christian interpreter, the canon will be the primary assigned realm.

For example, the interpreter can view the canonical first epistle of Paul to the Corinthians as being in the realm of *first-century Jewish letters*. Or it could be viewed as being in the realm of *first-century Greco-Roman letters*. You may notice that interpreters who assign 1 Corinthians to either one of these realms (perhaps without even realizing that they have done so) will naturally ask interpretive questions that align with this placement. Those who regard it as a *Jewish letter* will compare it to material by Philo or Josephus or other Jewish material, while those who regard it as a *Greco-Roman letter* will compare it to Seneca or others. These limitations are not necessarily problematic as long as they are recognized as resulting in limited findings.

Mission

We have seen that, in line with the emphasis on diversity mentioned earlier, the documents of the Bible can be seen as arising from a variety of missions. But as we have also seen, there is reason to think that in this variety we find polyphonic coherence. The main missions that are particularly relevant for the New Testament are the four directions of apostolic mission associated with

- Peter (apostle to the Jews)
- Paul (apostle to the Gentiles)
- John (associated with Ephesus)
- James (associated with Jerusalem)

A number of scholars consider this to be a fruitful way of thinking about all of the New Testament documents, though it is not a consensus opinion. The late E. Earle Ellis, who served at Southwest Baptist Theological Seminary, stated, "The making of the New Testament documents, with the exception of John's Gospel and letters, can be best explained as the contemporaneous activity of . . . four cooperating missions during one forty-year generation, i.e. AD 33–70."[1]

The following conception of the relation of New Testament documents to apostolic mission draws especially from Ellis:

LEADER	James	Peter	John	Paul
GOSPEL	Matthew	Mark	John	Luke [Acts]
LETTERS	James Jude	1 Peter 2 Peter	1 John 2 John 3 John Revelation	Romans 1 and 2 Corinthians Galatians Ephesians Philippians Colossians 1 and 2 Thessalonians 1 and 2 Timothy Titus Philemon [Hebrews]

---

[1] E. Earle Ellis, *The Making of the New Testament Documents* (Leiden: Brill, 1999), 330. As another example, see Paul Barnett, *Jesus and the Rise of Early Christianity* (Downers Grove, IL: IVP, 1999), 394.

Ellis himself believed that a reason for the overlap in content across different books of the New Testament (e.g., Jude and 2 Peter) is that the different missions cooperated in the use of preexisting traditions and in the ministry of key mission workers. Note that direct apostolic authorship is not assumed (so Acts and Hebrews), but rather, association with a particular apostolic mission team.

The interpreter might cautiously ask whether association with a particular direction of apostolic mission ought to influence the way we hear a particular book of the New Testament.

The book of 1 Corinthians clearly arises from the Pauline mission. It may be useful for the interpreter to give some consideration to this in priming for exegesis of the letter. One could look at 1 Thessalonians 1–2, which was written from Corinth, perhaps two years before 1 Corinthians was authored. According to this earlier letter, Paul considered his mission to be a ministry of the gospel of Jesus Christ, empowered by the Spirit. This gospel directed not only the content of Paul's message, but also his delivery and his lifestyle (1 Thess 2:4–8). The interpreter of 1 Corinthians would do well to consider how this broader Pauline mission of the gospel might have impacted Paul's letter: does Paul's gospel impact the style of his delivery in this letter? Does it impact the content?

Emergence

The New Testament emerged in the world of the first-century Mediterranean region. As with our discussion of the emergence of the Old Testament, we will give brief consideration to *geography*, *history*, *society*, and *literary conventions*.

Geography

It is important to have some awareness of the regions around the Mediterranean Sea in which the New Testament documents arose. For the Gospels, this means the primarily Jewish region of *Galilee*; the primarily Gentile region east of the Sea of Galilee, known as the *Decapolis*; the region of *Samaria*, south of Galilee; the region of *Judea*, south of Samaria, in which Jerusalem was located; and the region on the east of the Jordan River, known as *Perea*.

Galilee and Jerusalem are of particular significance, given that these are key locations for Jesus's ministry in the Gospels. Although perhaps known to us from the Old Testament as "Galilee of the Gentiles" (see 1 Maccabees 5:15; Matthew 4:15), archaeological artifacts indicate that by the time of the New Testament, Galilee was very similar to Judea in terms of its ethnic and religious makeup. One finds, for instance, plenty of examples of measures taken to ensure ritual purity, such as a prevalence of ritual baths and stone vessels (thought to allow water to remain pure for cleansing). Jerusalem had been a significant cosmopolitan city since the building projects of Herod the Great just before Jesus's birth. Its population expanded greatly at the time of the Jewish festivals, as pilgrims from Galilee and many other locations came to celebrate at the temple.

Even these basic facts are enough to aid interpretation of the Gospels. For example, the interpreter might ask whether it is significant that Mark's story of the feeding of the 5,000 occurred west of the Sea of Galilee (in Galilee), while the feeding of the 4,000 took place on the other side of the lake, in the (Gentile) region of the Decapolis. Or the interpreter might consider that the reason the people of the "city" (v. 10) had to inquire of "the crowds" (v. 11) as to the identity of the One making a triumphal entry into Jerusalem in Matthew 21 was that "the crowds" had accompanied Jesus on pilgrimage from Galilee, while the people of the "city" were the Jerusalemites themselves.

For the epistles, the regions of the Mediterranean that are north and west of these areas come into focus. At first, in the book of Acts, Syrian *Antioch* became a center of Christian mission, like *Jerusalem*. Following this, the areas of *Asia Minor* and *Europe* (Macedonia, Greece, and Rome) became significant.

Returning to our ongoing example of 1 Corinthians, it is useful to know that Corinth in the first century was a Roman city, which Julius Caesar refounded after, a century earlier, it had been destroyed. Its position as a port city meant that it had a thriving business center and was a major Greek hub.

History

Aside from issues of history behind the individual texts of the New Testament, the period between the biblical Testaments is of general importance.

The reign of *Media-Persia* lasted from 539 to 334 BC. With the conquests of Alexander, the reign of *Macedonia-Greece* (over Israel) lasted from 334 to 166 BC. After this, the Maccabean rebels successfully resisted Greek rule and instituted the *Jewish Hasmonean* kingdom from 143 to 63 BC. However, after a period of internal conflict, the general Pompey captured Jerusalem for *Roman* rule (63 BC–AD 135), though this did not mean immediate direct government in every region.

One of the key figures in this history was Antiochus IV Epiphanes. He was the Syrian Seleucid king in the 160s BC who sought to enforce Hellenization, but who was resisted and overthrown by the Maccabean rebels. The memory of the Maccabean martyrs, who died to preserve temple and Torah rather than eat unclean food or be uncircumcised, was strong in the time of the New Testament, and may illuminate some of the values of the Pharisees in particular.

In the Jewish rebellions against the Romans in the first century, many would have looked back to that former, successful, rebellion for inspiration. The destruction of Jerusalem in AD 70 was therefore a crushing defeat in more ways than one.

In terms of the significance of knowing history for the understanding of 1 Corinthians, it is crucial to recall, as mentioned earlier, that the Corinth of Paul's time was Roman in character and was not really the same city as had been there centuries before. For this reason, the oft-cited temple of Aphrodite with (supposedly) 1,000 cult prostitutes is irrelevant, being from the earlier, Greek city.

Society

As well as those elements of Jewish society seen in the postexilic period in the previous chapter, a number of other features are of general interest.

In terms of movements of popular Jewish devotion, Josephus reported that there were four "sects" of Judaism in the first century: the *Pharisees, Sadducees, Essenes,* and *Zealots.* While the Sadducees were aristocratic, the Essenes separatist, and the Zealots extremist, it was the Pharisees who had high regard among the general Jewish population, being concerned for the purity and righteousness of the people as a whole.

In terms of politics and religion across the various regions of the New Testament era, it is important to recognize the pervasive impacts and values of the *Roman Empire.* While, in my view, the significance of the Roman Empire has been overplayed in recent discussion of the New Testament, it remains an essential background. The stability that was forcibly brought upon the Mediterranean region by the Roman superpower resulted in both resentment and attraction for the people affected. In terms of the four sects of Judaism Josephus identified, each responded to Roman rule in a distinct way. To simplify, the Pharisees pursued *purification*, the Sadducees pursued *accommodation*, the Essenes pursued *separation*, and the Zealots pursued *retaliation*.

To return to our example of 1 Corinthians, the interpreter could ask: Are Roman conventions of honor and patronage behind the community's pride in the sinful man of chapter 5? What were Roman conventions of head covering, and how do these illuminate chapter 11? Might people attracted to Roman social mobility have been inclined to take particular views on resurrection?

Literary conventions

Numerous genres appear in the New Testament. We will consider key exegetical questions to ask when we encounter the terms *Gospel, epistle,* and *apocalyptic.*

Richard Burridge has argued vigorously that the *Gospels* of the New Testament are recognizably ancient *bioi*—"Lives," such as those we might find in other first-century authors, like Plutarch. However, he argues, they represent a subgenre of that broad category, with their own characteristics: *bioi Iesou*—"Lives of Jesus."[2] This perspective has received some challenges and qualifications, but has been largely persuasive: the Gospels of the New Testament carry structures and themes that are reminiscent of Greco-Roman "Lives"—most notably the focus on a *person* rather than on abstract concepts. But they also appear to carry generic qualities of Old Testament Scripture, apparently being influenced by narrative books of the Hebrew Bible.[3] Numerous questions present themselves as useful, many of which are the same as for Old Testament narrative:

1. How does the passage fit into a larger plot development?

2. Are there devices (such as repeated plot markers or locational shifts or *inclusio*) that indicate the parameters of a particular section?

3. How might the passage be divided into "scenes"?

4. Why was each event selected for inclusion? What does it add to the story being told? Are certain events given more space than others? Why? Are certain events left out? Why?

5. Are any details labored redundantly? Why might this be the case?

6. What does the passage leave ambiguous? What does it ensure is unambiguous?

7. Is this Gospel written to encourage believers or to evangelize unbelievers?

8. How does this Gospel relate to the others? Consider the impacts of the Synoptic question and the evangelist's use of sources: is Matthew adding to Mark's scene in a particular way?

Although there are certainly other first-century letters written in Greek, the attempt to compare them with *New Testament epistles* has not been as fruitful as might be hoped. This is because the New Testament letters are generally much longer than other letters of the time, and the progression of their contents does not seem to follow a prescribed flow (apart from openings and closings). Comparison with speech rhetoric of the era has been controversial, and—in my view—not very productive. Nevertheless, numerous exegetical questions will generally be helpful for the interpreter:

---

[2] R. Burridge, *What Are the Gospels? A Comparison with Graeco-Roman Biography*, 2nd ed. (Grand Rapids: Eerdmans, 2004).

[3] See, for example, Roland Deines, "Did Matthew Know He Was Writing Scripture? Part 1," *European Journal of Theology* 22, no. 2 (2013): 101–9; "Did Matthew Know He Was Writing Scripture? Part 2," *European Journal of Theology* 23, no. 1 (2014): 3–12.

1. What can we know about the recipients? For example, were they largely Gentile? Were they familiar with the Old Testament?

2. What do we know about the sender and co-sender(s)?

3. Is there a logical argument that can be discerned?

4. Is the structure illumined by other New Testament letters, or ancient conventions, or the gospel itself?

5. What impacts could we imagine this passage having on its first hearers? Might it have had the effect of shaming them? Encouraging them? Making them indignant? Calming their anxieties?

New Testament Apocalyptic is seen most extensively in the book of Revelation. This style of literature (of which there are numerous extrabiblical examples) was especially used by Jewish writers in situations of oppression. Material using this genre sought to assure hearers that behind the brutal scenes of history, God was at work, preparing a future in which justice will be done. The genre is characterized by vivid imagery and symbolism, drawing on inner-cultural conventions to communicate an exhortation to resolute perseverance. Several questions will be particularly useful for the book of Revelation:

1. Are there images (e.g., lamb, lampstands, olive trees) that resonate with more straightforward literary material in the rest of the Johannine literature? In the rest of the New Testament? In the Old Testament?

2. What features of a letter are evident? In what ways might these particular recipients have heard the work?

3. In what ways might this passage have encouraged perseverance among persecuted Ephesian Christians?

4. How is the Johannine gospel evident in this work?

Reception

The reception of the New Testament involves 2,000 years of interpretation and cultural impacts. For those engaging in academic exegesis, there is a particular expectation that attention will be given to the reception of New Testament texts in settings of academic interpretation (such as commentaries and journal articles). However, other areas of reception are also important. Here we will briefly consider some features of the earliest centuries of reception, in which we witness the rise of Christian doctrine, the rise of Christian practice, and the recognition of Christian canon.

The rise of Christian doctrine

Anglican theologian Gerald Bray argues[4] that the impacts of the New Testament on patristic hearers indicate that the New Testament materials were not merely read as contingent and occasional, but were seen to suggest theology proper: knowledge of God. Bray has proposed that the Fathers regarded the Bible as a theological unity that testifies to ontological realities—supremely, God himself as Trinity. This, he pointed out, can be thought of as an important critical voice for modern biblical scholarship, which frequently detects theological development throughout a historically diverse canon.

This is an important point: the Bible, and the New Testament in particular, drove early Christians to create creeds in times of theological controversy to summarize historic orthodoxy. And these creeds focused on the nature and persons of God.

Of course, there were other factors at work in the development of these creeds (such as the influence of Greek philosophy). Nevertheless, this theological footprint of the New Testament in the time of the patristics needs to be taken into account in any consideration of the New Testament's reception: it was received in a manner that lent itself to propositional declarations concerning the being and work of God.

The rise of Christian practice

As well as the impacts of the New Testament on Christian belief, it is important to note the impacts of the New Testament on Christian behavior. In the field of New Testament Christology, for example, historian Larry Hurtado finds it significant that the Christ event, attested from a variety of witnesses, prompted worship of Christ alongside God the Father. This can be seen in such devotional practices as early songs and the adoption of certain scribal conventions for names of both God and Jesus.[5] Other practices, such as asceticism or institutionalization are also worthy of consideration.

The recognition of Christian canon

If an early Christian text under consideration came to be recognized as canonical Scripture, or came to be rejected as heretical or non-apostolic, this is a feature of its reception that is important to take into account.

---

[4] Gerald Bray, "The Church Fathers and Biblical Theology" in Craig Bartholomew et al., eds., *Out of Egypt: Biblical Theology and Biblical Interpretation*, Scripture and Hermeneutics 5 (Milton Keynes, UK: Paternoster, 2004), 23–40.

[5] See especially Larry W. Hurtado, *The Earliest Christian Artifacts* (Grand Rapids: Eerdmans, 2006).

Of course, in all of these areas, reception is not a sure guide to inherent meaning of the texts under consideration, but it is worthy of attention.

In terms of 1 Corinthians, one feature of its reception that is worth noticing—although it is perhaps more recent than the general features we have considered—is its remarkably tenacious presence in weddings. First Corinthians 13 is used in thousands of weddings, worldwide, every week. Although the interpreter might be tempted to brush this off as ignorant misuse, such pervasive cultural resonance should not be ignored: why does this chapter find such a warm welcome in these sorts of celebratory settings? What might that tell us about the chapter itself?

The New Testament as Christian Scripture

Theology, Canon, Gospel

As we saw in the previous chapter, the refined (but provisional) theological pre-understanding that the Christian interpreter brings to the Bible finds the boundaries of polyphony in the canon, and the center of its coherence in the gospel of Jesus Christ. It will be fruitful to spend some time considering how these elements will impact Christian interpretation of the New Testament.

While I stated earlier that the New Testament documents are, from one perspective, examples of "early Christian literature," for *Christian* interpretation the canon of books that came to be recognized as Scripture provides a primary realm. The New Testament canon is built upon, and brings fulfilment to, the Old Testament canon. This will need to be brought into conscious consideration in interpretive examination: in what ways does *this* text contribute to the function of the New Testament as attesting fulfillment of the eschatological orientation of the Old Testament?

Looking again at 1 Corinthians, one could ask where Paul got his image of the "rulers of this age" (2:6, 8) and consider the resonances between Daniel 2 and 1 Corinthians 1–2: what biblical themes and characters are developed, and how should this impact Christian hearers?

It will be fruitful for the interpreter to consider whether the New Testament passage under consideration might serve the broad Christian mission of declaring Jesus Christ to be the One who tames hostile powers and rises to the right hand of God. But as I have suggested elsewhere, the Christian interpreter will read the texts from the vantage point of *participation* in this mission, rather than just analysis of New Testament mission:

One who is shaped by the cross is particularly attuned and open to the formational orientation of the kerygma, whether explicit or implicit. We see this illustrated in Mark's gospel, where James and John are shown to be unable to understand Jesus and his kingdom. Jesus says to them, "You do not know what you are asking. Are you able to drink the cup that I drink, or be baptized with the baptism that I am baptized with?" (Mark 10:38). Then, in contrast to these cruciphobic, glory-thirsty disciples, Mark immediately presents us with an ideal disciple who can truly *understand*: the blind beggar, Bartimaeus. He understands who Jesus is, and he understands that a true disciple will cast off the past, and follow Jesus to the place of his execution. Jesus seeks interpreters such as these.[6]

This brings us back to the point at which this book began: the hermeneutical goal of biblical interpretation is not simply "recovery of meaning," but the refining listening of softhearted disciples who are being transformed.

An Exegetical Case Study: 1 Corinthians 13:1–3

From Live Exegesis to Exegesis Paper

In the last chapter, I offered some live exegesis, showing the sorts of exploratory questions that I would begin to ask as a primed interpreter of 1 Samuel 17. In this chapter, I will offer an "exegesis paper," of the sort that might be required in a university or seminary academic setting. I have followed the structure suggested in chapter 8 and keep to a 1,000-word limit. I made use of the Greek text, but use transliterations here.

You will notice that the areas of *priming*, while evident, are not the focus. The focus is the language of the text itself. And the *refining* exegetical questions have now become implicit, rather than being spelled out. That is, rather than explicitly asking, "What do readers from other cultures make of this verse?" or "How is the passage structured?" I simply demonstrate my findings about these sorts of questions as relevant.

There are a few other features of this style of academic writing that you might notice. For one thing, I have attempted to be economical with words. I avoided long, elaborate introductory comments because I wanted to give as much space as possible to substantial analysis. The tone is relatively formal, but I did attempt

---

[6] Matthew R. Malcolm, "Biblical Hermeneutics and *Kerygmatic* Responsibility," in Porter and Malcolm, *Future of Biblical Interpretation*, 63 (see chap. 4, n. 18).

at points to demonstrate that this comes from a located interpreter, rather than a pseudo-objective robot. I did not comment on every grammatical feature—only those that are particularly important for my interpretation of the passage. I referenced secondary literature in order to interact with it, not simply to back up my own assertions. At the same time, I was rigorously guided by attention to the primary text itself in terms of the substance and flow of the exegesis.

Having said all this, a 1,000-word limit is extremely brief. If I had more space, I would pursue deeper analysis of each clause and more thorough engagement with current scholarship.

Exegesis Paper on 1 Corinthians 13:1–3

Approaching the text

Within the flow of the letter, chapters 12–14 represent yet another example of Corinthian pride that Paul seeks to subvert with the impacts of the cross. Here it is pride in spiritual manifestations. As in several other parts of the letter, the broad section carries an ABA' pattern, with chapter 13 being the B section, transitioning from an argument that all believers are gifted by the Spirit for mutual service (chapter 12), through to the specific case of tongues and prophecy (chapter 14). Chapter 13 eloquently (and ironically) urges that the most superior "way" (12:31) is that of love. The chapter is saturated with key terminology from the rest of the letter, indicating that love is one spiritual "possession" that appears all too lacking in Corinth.

The chapter falls naturally into three parts: 1–3 (on gifts without love); 4–7 (on what love is and is not); and 8–13 (on what will last).

Observing the text

Using memorably "structured prose,"[7] Paul presents a hypothetical situation (using the subjunctive mood), pushing to hyperbolic extremes the sorts of gifts that the Corinthians are apparently proud to manifest.

As Aquinas noticed,[8] Paul seems to depict three categories of gifts: first, those that relate to speech (13:1); second, those that relate to knowledge (13:2); and third, those that relate to works (13:3). That the gifts are grouped into three is evident from the threefold *agapan de mē echo*. The use of representative triads in 1 Corinthians is frequent (e.g., 1:26, 30; 3:12; 12:4–6), so one might be cautious about the precise significance of these three categories. It does seem that "speaking"

---

[7] Joseph Fitzmyer, *First Corinthians* (New Haven, CT: Yale University Press, 2008), 487.

[8] Aquinas, *Commentary on 1 Corinthians*, sec. 759 (see chap. 2, n. 39).

and "knowledge" are especially at issue in Corinth (8:1–3; 12:1–3), and a similar ordering of categories appears to come at the beginning of the letter (1:4–9), in which Paul thanks God for the Corinthians' riches in speech, knowledge, and fullness of gifting. However, the threefold categorical division should not be pressed: Paul will later (13:8–9) utilize the slightly different triad of tongues, knowledge, and prophecy, in contrast with the triad of faith, hope, and love.

In each of these three verses, the subordinate clause is prioritized, coming before the main verb. This establishes a frame of reference for the verb, but also carries the rhetorical effect of drawing attention to the prized gifts before surprisingly removing their value. This rhetorical effect is heightened by the use of the first-person singular throughout: in each case, the gifts that are prized are raised in the persona of Paul to improbably extreme levels (tongues *of angels*; understanding *all mysteries*; giving up one's body *to be burned*), before revealing that even at this extremity of apparent spiritual manifestation, the gifts are worthless without love.

Intriguingly, *agapē* is treated here as a possession (*mē echo*) rather than an action or attribute. This may be in ironic correlation to Corinthian boasting in "possessing" certain gifts, such as knowledge (8:1: *gnosin echomen*), healing, or tongues (12:30: *mē pantes charismata echousin iamaton? Mē pantes glossais lalousin?* Cf. 7:40 for a similar ironic use).

Verse 1

The gift of tongues was conspicuously left to the ends of the lists of gifts in chapter 12 and is introduced as the first item here. As numerous commentators throughout history have noted,[9] this is undoubtedly because Paul is seeking to undermine the misplaced Corinthian pride in tongues that he will address more directly in chapter 14. The reference to angels fits with Paul's pattern of hyperbole, rather than representing a Corinthian claim (against Fee).

Some commentators detect a reference to pagan worship in the clanging cymbal.[10] This is possible, though it may simply be an example of indistinct or non-communicative sound (cf. 14:7–8; Mark 5:38).

---

[9] Ibid., sec. 760; Robert D. Sider (ed.), *Collected Works of Erasmus, vol 43: Paraphrases on the Epistles to the Corinthians, Ephesians, Philippians, Colossians, and Thessalonians* (University of Toronto Press, 2009), 157; Gordon D. Fee, *The First Epistle to the Corinthians* (Grand Rapids: Eerdmans, 2014), 698.

[10] As a reader who has spent most of his life in highly secular Australia, I note with interest that commentators in both the *Africa Bible Commentary* and the *South Asia Bible Commentary* detect a negative reference to pagan worship in the mention of cymbals (pages 1419 and 1577, respectively).

Verse 2

The gift of *propheteia* was perhaps thought of in Corinth as one of the two main "spirituals" (12:1; cf. Acts 19:6) and was clearly practiced there (11:4; 14:3). It seems to be linked here to the attaining of mysteries and knowledge, both of which have also previously come up in the letter (4:1; 8:1). This suggests, against the interpolation theory of William O. Walker,[11] that this chapter is related to the rest of the letter in addressing the Corinthian situation.

The mention of moving a mountain is proverbial (Mark 11:23) and serves as another example of hyperbole.

Verse 3

The main textual problem in this verse (*kauthēsomai* or *kauchēsomai*) is difficult to judge on external grounds. Two internal considerations are important. First, it is conceivable that a scribe might accidentally give the reading "to boast," given that this theme (using this verb and cognates) is prevalent in the letter (1:31; 3:21; 4:7; 5:6; 9:15–16; 15:31). Second, the rhetorical patterning of the passage makes better sense if the "giving over of the body" is for the sake of hyperbolic good works (so the martyrdom of being burned) rather than for the sake of boasting—in which case it would be no surprise for love to be absent.

BIG IDEA

Interpretation of the New Testament involves giving attention to specific features of the New Testament's locatedness, as well as recognizing its special status as Christian Scripture. Exegesis of the New Testament (as of the Old Testament) ought to involve close attention to the text itself, in a way that is informed about the locatedness of the Bible and the reader.

Interacting with the Text

That this text is a beloved passage for weddings attests that Paul's language is beautifully poetic. What this feature of the passage's reception perhaps misses is its devastatingly eloquent subversion of stubborn Corinthian pride. In my own setting, I am struck that if I have exegetical skills to silence opponents, but have not love, I am nothing. Exegesis will pass away, but faith, hope, and love will remain.

---

11 William O. Walker, Jr. *Interpolations in the Pauline Letters* (London: A&C Black, 2001).

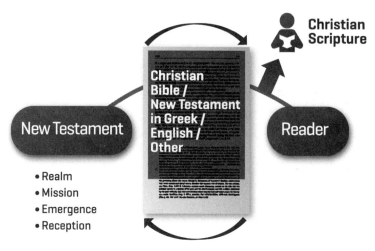

Figure 8.

Questions for Discussion

1. What are some valid "realms" that a reader might posit for the New Testament documents?

2. Does the New Testament arise from a united apostolic mission? If so, how would you describe the mission of the apostles?

3. What are the most important features of the emergence of the New Testament documents in the first century?

4. What have been some fruitful directions in the reception history of the New Testament? What directions would you want to critique?

5. How would you evaluate the exegesis paper on 1 Corinthians in this chapter? Did it show respect for the "locatedness" of the author? Did it acknowledge the "locatedness" of the exegete? Did it fairly address the text?

6. How can you develop your own exegetical skills? What areas could you work on?

For Further Reading

Blomberg, Craig L., and Jennifer Foutz Markley. 2010. *A Handbook of New Testament Exegesis.* Grand Rapids: Baker Academic.

Erickson, Richard J. 2005. *A Beginner's Guide to New Testament Exegesis.* Downers Grove, IL: IVP.

Fee, Gordon D. 2002. *New Testament Exegesis: A Handbook for Students and Pastors.* Third edition. Louisville: Westminster John Knox Press.

Green, Joel, ed. 2010. *Hearing the New Testament: Strategies for Interpretation.* Second edition. Grand Rapids: Eerdmans.

EPILOGUE

Through reading this book, it is inevitable that you will have come to know me a little better—by the end of the book, the attentive reader will have picked up that I have a wife and children, that I (used to!) have chickens, that I did a doctoral dissertation on 1 Corinthians, that I am Christian, that I do not identify as homosexual, that I am mystified by abstract theater, that I am fascinated by Bede, that I teach university students, that I used to live in Australia but now live in Indonesia, and so on. This is entirely appropriate—and quite intentional—for a book on hermeneutics, because this is not a book by a disinterested robot; it is a book by a particular someone, located in a specific place and time, with individual horizons of understanding. I hope that as you engage with this work, you will recognize that you too are located in a particular place and time, and that this recognition of mutual locatedness will result in a meaningful and transforming encounter.

So, what am I hoping will result from this encounter? What am I hoping that you will take from this book?

I hope you will recognize that hermeneutics is the study of what is happening when effective interpretation or understanding takes place. I hope you will agree that biblical exegesis involves a consciously located interpreter questioning a particular text, in thoughtful awareness of dimensions of locatedness of the biblical other, resulting in a rigorous, respectful interpretation of the text. And I hope that you will put into practice the movement "from hermeneutics to exegesis" that involves conducting interpretation with one's eyes open to what is going on in the process.

In particular, if you are a Christian interpreter, then I hope you will allow historic Christian convictions to direct the way you approach the Bible, while being informed by what general hermeneutics tells us about human understanding. This means—at some point in the interpretive process—consciously acting on the faithful Christian prejudice that the biblical documents belong in the "realm" of Christian Scripture, while also being able to posit, listen to, or interact with alternative realms for the biblical documents. Most of all, I hope that your careful attention to the text will draw you closer to the One who said, "Pay attention to what you hear. By the measure you use, it will be measured to you—and more will be added to you" (Mark 4:24).

NAME INDEX

A

Adam, A. K. M.   *55*
Ayres, Lewis   *15*

B

Baglow, Christopher T.   *93*
Bailey, James L.   *125*
Bakhtin, M. M.   *90*
Barnett, Paul   *152*
Barth, Karl   *57–58*
Bartholomew, Craig G.   *10, 47, 53–55, 80*
Barton, John   *150*
Bates, Matthew W.   *99–100*
Bauckham, Richard   *121–122*
Berding, Kenneth   *138*
Bergen, Benjamin K.   *62, 63, 77*
Black, David Alan   *110*
Bouma, Jeremy   *4*
Bray, Gerald   *158*
Briggs, Richard S.   *150*
Brown, Jeannine   *88*
Bühler, Karl   *18, 73*
Burridge, R.   *125, 155, 156*
Byargeon, Rick   *136*

C

Calvin, John   *29–31, 47, 57, 59, 90, 95, 101, 138*
Campbell, Constantine   *111, 128*
Carson, D. A.   *49, 52, 116*

Chase

Chase, Frederic Henry   *58*
Childs, Brevard S.   *94*
Chrysostom, John   *20–21, 67*

D

Deines, Roland   *121, 156*
Dilthey, W.   *31–36, 38, 45*
Dodd, C. H.   *96*
Dunn, James   *120*

E

Edsall, Benjamin A.   *96–99*
Ehrman, Bart   *83, 121*
Ellis, Earle, E.   *152, 153*

F

Fairbairn, Donald   *16*
Fee, Gordon D.   *4, 162–164*
Finley, Thomas J.   *110*
Fitzmyer, Joseph   *161*
Fowl, Stephen E.   *48–49*
Frame, John M.   *60*
Franke, John R.   *141*

G

Gadamer, Hans-Georg   *4, 8–9, 12, 14, 21, 35–40, 45–47, 61, 65–67, 79, 118*
Gander, Hans-Helmuth   *10*
Gillingham, Susan   *28–30*

167

SUBJECT INDEX

SCRIPTURE INDEX